Childcraft
The How and Why Library

Volume 11

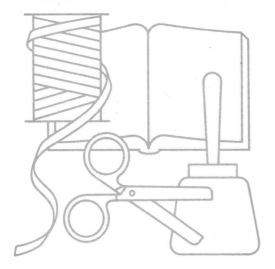

Make and Do

Field Enterprises Educational Corporation

Chicago Frankfurt London Paris Rome Sydney Tokyo Toronto

A subsidiary of
Field Enterprises, Inc.

Volume 11

Make and Do

Contents

Most of the things to make and do in this volume can be put together from bits and scraps you find around the house. Here are some of the ordinary materials and tools called for in this book. But the editors encourage your imagination and judgment in suiting the projects and materials to your needs, and to what you have available.

aluminum foil	needle	scissors
balloon	paints	shellac
buttons	paper	soap
cardboard	paper bag	spool
cardboard box	paper clips	string
cloth	paper plate	tape
clothespins	paste or glue	thread
crayons	pencil	thumbtack
crepe paper	pins	tin can
drinking straw	pipe cleaner	toothpicks
flour	rubber band	wax paper
hammer and nails	ruler	wood
modeling clay	salt	yarn

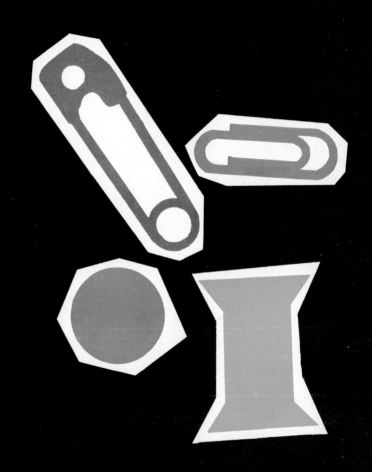

fun with odds and ends

Is there an old paper bag around the house? Are there any tin cans, pop bottles, string? Don't throw them away. You can make toys from all kinds of odds and ends. On the next pages are easy-to-make toys that are fun to play with.

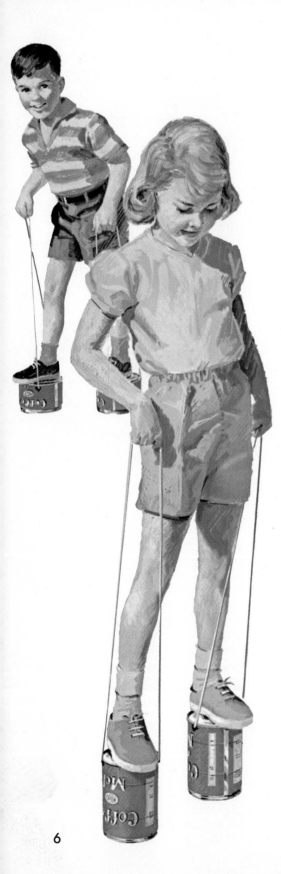

Tin-Can Stilts

Materials

- 2 cans of the same size
- hammer and nail
- scissors
- 2 pieces of string, each about as tall as you are

Punch a nail hole on each side of the unopened ends of the cans. See Picture.

Thread a string through the holes in each can. Tie knots so the string won't pull through. The knotted ends should be inside the cans. Stand on top of the cans. Pull the strings up.

Hold the strings tight and walk.

You can make tin-can stilts with taller cans, and then still taller cans.

Building

Sand Castles

With Cans

Materials

- all sizes and shapes of tin cans
- adhesive tape for any rough edges

Ask your mother to save tin cans of different shapes. Ask her to help you be sure *both* top and bottom lids are off.

Tape edges with adhesive tape.

Now you are ready to build sand and block castles. Set the can on the sand. Fill it with wet sand. Then lift the can carefully, leaving the sand smoothly shaped like the inside of the can. Each can will make its own shape. A flat can will make a boat shape. A tall, round can will make a castle tower.

Boats
From
Walnut
Shells

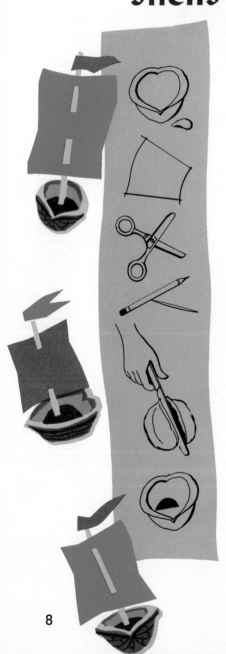

Materials
- an unbroken half of a walnut shell
- clay
- a piece of paper
- blunt scissors
- a pencil
- toothpicks

Carefully cut a walnut shell in half.

Put a small wad of clay inside of it.

Draw a sail about the size of a postage stamp and cut it out. Put a toothpick mast in and out through the sail. See Picture. Stick the bottom end of the mast in the clay.

Your boat is ready to sail. You can make several boats and have races.

Cork Floaters

Materials
- a large cork stopper • blunt scissors
- cardboard • a thumbtack • crayons

Use only half of a cork stopper for each floater. Ask Mother or Dad to cut the cork stopper in half. You can make two floating toys out of one cork.

Lay one cork half on its flat side. In the center of the rounded side, cut a small slit. This slit will hold the cardboard cutout.

Draw a duck on cardboard with a small tab at the bottom. The tab will fit in the slit of the cork.

Color the duck on both sides with wax crayons to waterproof it. Cut it out and stick the tab in the slit. Stick a thumbtack on the cork to weight it.

You can make all kinds of cork floaters. The other half of the cork is waiting.

9

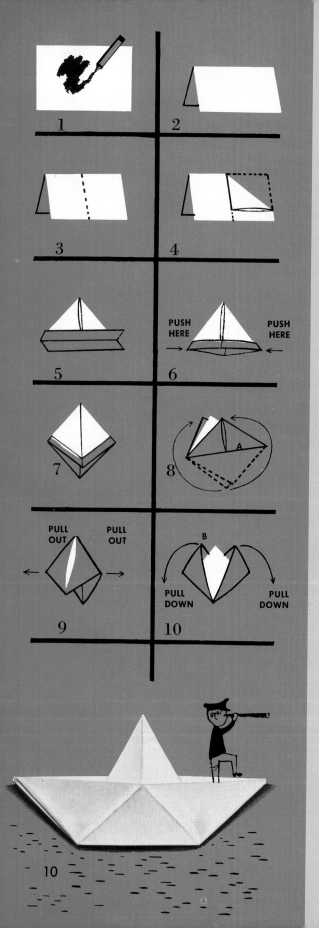

PAPER SAILING SHIP

Materials
- a sheet of paper, a little larger than this page
- wax crayons
- blunt scissors

Make a hat, pull on the corners, and surprise—a waterproof boat.

1. Color a sheet of paper on both sides with crayons to waterproof.

2. Fold it in half the long way.

3. Open the paper and fold it in half the short way.

4. Take one of the two corners along the fold, and fold it into the center crease. Do the same with the other corner.

5. Turn up the end flaps.

6. Cut the corners off the flaps, and you have a hat.

7. Press the end folds of the hat together so that the middle creases become the outside folds.

8. Fold the bottom points up in the peak.

9. Again press the end folds together so that the middle creases become the outside folds, as in Step 7.

10. At the top of your folded square, three corner points come together to form one corner. Hold the two outside ones and pull them away from the middle point. Press down on the sides to complete your boat.

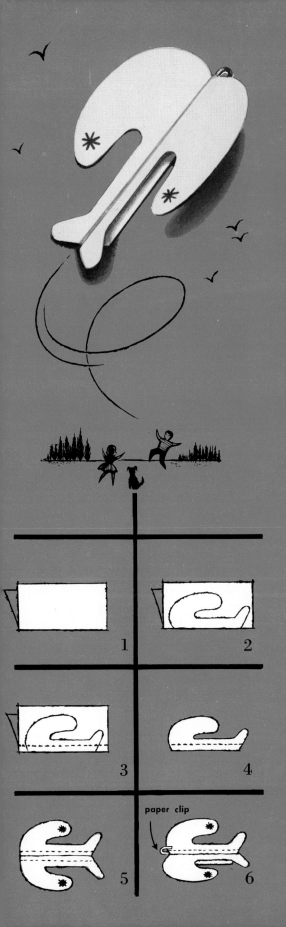

LOOP-the-LOOP
PAPER PLANE

Materials
- a sheet of heavy paper
- a pencil
- blunt scissors
- a paper clip
- crayons

Here's a paper airplane that will fly in circles.

1. Fold the paper in half the long way.

2. Draw an airplane with wings and a tail on it. See Picture.

3. Draw a line about an inch away from the fold on each side the full length of the paper. See Picture.

4. Cut out the airplane, but do not cut on the fold.

5. Spread out the airplane and color. You can draw airplane markings near each wing tip.

6. Refold your airplane. Now fold each wing down along the line drawn on it.

7. Add a paper clip to the nose.

You can change the way your airplane flies by changing the wing shape and putting more than one paper clip on the nose.

11

SQUIRMY

Materials

- empty spools
- yarn or string
- poster paint and a brush
- shellac
- a button, a milk-bottle cap, or a clothespin

To find out how much string or yarn you need for Squirmy, put your spools in a straight line. You will need string that is about three or four times as long as your row of spools.

Leave a small piece at one end of your string for a tail, and then tie a big knot. The knot will keep the spools from falling off.

String your spools. If you have beads, string them between the spools. Leave some room on the string for Squirmy to move around—about as much room as two spools would take up—and tie another big knot. This knot will keep the spools from sliding off the front.

The string that's left will be your puller.

If you want a good puller, tie a button or clothespin or milk-bottle cap to the end of the puller string.

You might paint or decorate Squirmy. If you shellac it, the colors will stay bright.

STRINGING SPOOLS

Materials
- empty spools, any size will do
- yarn or cord
- tempera paint and brush
- shellac

Paint your spools bright colors. Use shellac to keep them shiny.

Decide whether you want to make a spool necklace or a spool belt. Cut a piece of yarn or cord. Be sure it's a little longer than the amount you need to go around your neck or waist, so you'll have some extra for tying.

To keep the spools from sliding off, tie a large knot at one end of the yarn. String the spools. When all the spools are on, tie the two yarn ends together.

For some unusual spool stringing, try using buttons or beads between the spools. You can also make colorful necklaces and belts by using buttons or beads or both.

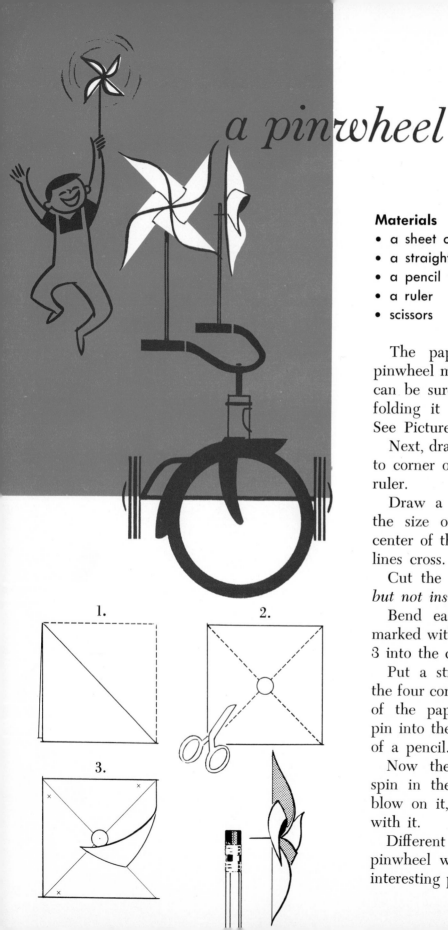

a pinwheel

Materials
- a sheet of paper
- a straight pin
- a pencil with an eraser
- a ruler
- scissors

The paper that makes a pinwheel must be square. You can be sure it is a square by folding it before you cut it. See Picture 1.

Next, draw lines from corner to corner of the paper with a ruler.

Draw a small circle about the size of a penny in the center of the paper where the lines cross. See Picture 2.

Cut the paper on the lines *but not inside the circle.*

Bend each of the corners marked with an "X" in Picture 3 into the center of the circle.

Put a straight pin through the four corners and the center of the paper. Then put the pin into the eraser on the end of a pencil.

Now the pinwheel should spin in the wind, when you blow on it, or when you run with it.

Different decorations on a pinwheel will make new and interesting patterns as it spins.

1.

2.

3.

Materials

- a sharpened pencil stub
- a nail to punch a hole
- scissors
- cardboard
- crayons

spin top, spin!

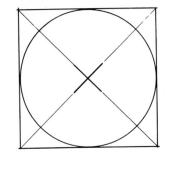

Draw a circle on cardboard. You might use the rim of a drinking glass for a pattern. Cut the circle out.

Decorate the circle with bright crayon designs.

Punch a hole in the center of the circle with a nail.

Stick the sharpened pencil stub through the hole just as far as it shows in the Picture. Now you have a top that will spin.

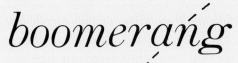

boomerang

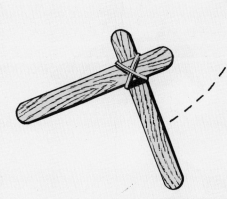

Materials

- 2 ice-cream sticks   • a thread or a rubber band

Cross two ice-cream sticks the way the sticks are crossed in the picture. Tie them in this position with a thread or a rubber band.

Toss the boomerang with a flick of your wrist so that it spins. It will come back to you.

15

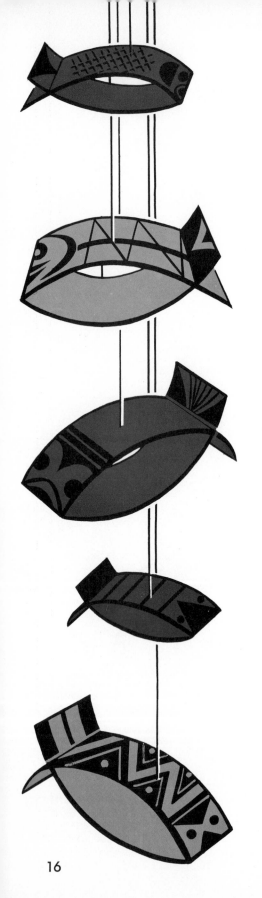

A FISH TO HANG UP

Materials
- construction paper
- ruler
- blunt scissors
- string

1. With a ruler draw a straight line two inches away from the long side of a piece of construction paper. Then take your scissors, cut along the line you have drawn, and you'll have a long strip of paper.

2. Fold it in half, and crease it. Then one inch from one end of the strip, cut through the paper from the side halfway across, as shown in the picture. On the other end, cut halfway across the paper from the other side.

3. Now bring both ends together, and fit the cuts together. The fan at the end forms the fish's tail.

4. Poke a small hole in the fish's back, and push a piece of string through the hole. Knot the end of the string so it won't pull through the paper. You can draw eyes and mouth on your fish, if you wish. Then hang it up.

You can make many fish of different colored paper, and hang them in your room.

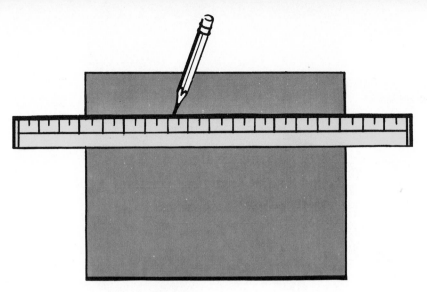

1. Draw line. Then, cut.

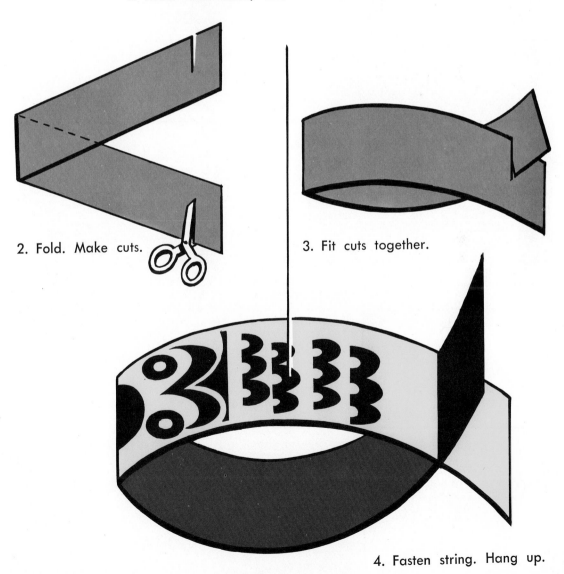

2. Fold. Make cuts.

3. Fit cuts together.

4. Fasten string. Hang up.

Bookmarks

MY BOOK
Jeanne Jones

animal bookmarks

Cut a strip of cardboard about three fingers wide and a little shorter than your book.

Draw an animal with a big face on one end of the cardboard strip. Color it and cut around it. The body of the animal is the rest of the cardboard.

Slip the bookmark between the pages of your book at the place that you want to mark.

funny bookmarks

Cut a narrow strip of crepe paper and wind it on a slant round and round your stick or piece of cardboard. Paste down the end.

On a separate piece of paper, draw eyes, ears, nose, and mouth. Cut them out and paste them in place for a face. A funny beard, glasses, earrings, a big tie, or a hat can be added. Cut out a dress or suit and paste it on.

Or make cartoon bookmarks by cutting out pictures of your favorite funny paper characters and pasting them on the cardboard or stick.

bookplates

Bookplates are labels that you paste in your books to tell people that the books belong to you.

Cut a piece of tape as wide as your hand. Leave a big place in the middle for your name, and draw a design around it. Paint the design on the bookplate with bright colors. Carefully print or write your name on it.

Wet the back of your bookplate and stick it on the inside cover of your book.

MAKING MUSICAL INSTRUMENTS

Bang! Clink! Ping! Ting!

These are the sounds made by gongs, triangles, and xylophones.

A Gong

Materials

- a lid of a large popcorn or potato-chip can   • a knife or a spoon for a mallet   • a nail   • a hammer   • a string

Ask your father to help you pound two nail holes into the rim of the lid. They should be a few inches apart.

Thread a string through the holes. Tie the ends of the string together. You can hold the gong by this string. See Picture.

Use a knife or a spoon as the mallet for striking the gong. You might want to wrap a strip of cloth around the hitting end of the mallet to make a softer tone when you hit the gong.

A Triangle

Materials

- a short length of metal pipe or a horseshoe
- a string   • a knife, a fork, or a spoon for a mallet

A triangle, like a gong, is held by a string. Use a piece of string three times as long as the pipe. Run the string through the pipe and tie the ends of the string together.

Hold it as shown in the picture. Strike it with a knife, a fork, or a spoon.

If you use a horseshoe instead of a pipe for the triangle, tie only one end of the string to the curve of the horseshoe. You can then strike the horseshoe as it hangs from the string.

A Xylophone

Materials

- empty pop bottles or water glasses
- a knife, a fork, or a spoon for a mallet

Collect several old pop bottles. It is best if they are all the same size and shape. Fill one bottle with water nearly to the top. Fill the second one halfway. Put just a little water in the third. Put other amounts of water in the other bottles.

Now hit each bottle gently with a piece of kitchen silver.

You can change the sound of each bottle by changing the amount of water in it. By experimenting with different amounts of water, you will be able to sound notes in tune with a piano.

If you do not have pop bottles, ask your mother if she will let you use some water glasses.

A Hummer

Materials

- an empty paper-roll tube
- wax paper   • a rubber band   • crayons or paints

Cut out a circle of wax paper larger than the end of a paper-role tube. Put the paper circle over the end of the tube. Fasten it in place with a rubber band.

Sing *O-O-O-O* into the open end of the tube.

You can decorate the hummer in any way you like with crayons or paints.

Hum On A Comb

Wrap a sheet of tissue paper around a comb and hum into it.

You can feel the paper vibrate against your lips. It tickles a little when you hum, but it makes a good band instrument.

21

HOW TO MAKE DRUMS

Boom! Boom! Boom! There are many kinds of drums.
Bongo drums! Kettledrums! Tom-toms!
Here's how to make a tom-tom
and a bongo drum.

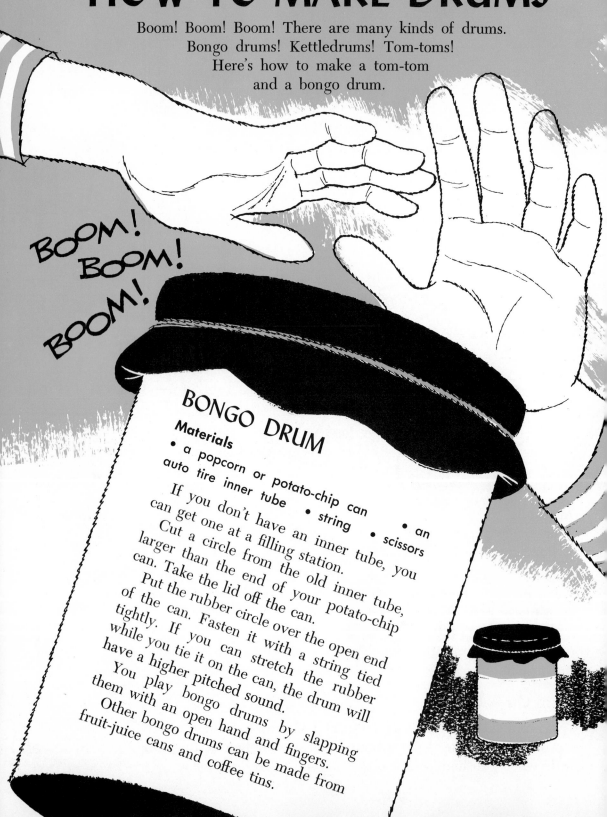

BOOM!
BOOM!
BOOM!

BONGO DRUM

Materials

- a popcorn or potato-chip can
- an auto tire inner tube
- string
- scissors

If you don't have an inner tube, you can get one at a filling station.

Cut a circle from the old inner tube, larger than the end of your potato-chip can. Take the lid off the can.

Put the rubber circle over the open end of the can. Fasten it with a string tied tightly. If you can stretch the rubber while you tie it on the can, the drum will have a higher pitched sound.

You play bongo drums by slapping them with an open hand and fingers.

Other bongo drums can be made from fruit-juice cans and coffee tins.

TOM-TOM
Materials
- a large, round cereal carton
- string
- something to punch holes
- clothespins

Remove the lid from a round cereal carton. Just below the open end, punch a hole in the side of the carton. Punch another hole directly opposite the first. Run a string through the holes and tie the ends. You can now hang the box around your neck. Put the lid back on the carton.

If you wish, you can decorate the cereal box with poster paints. You can also tape the lid to the carton to keep it on.

Use clothespins for drumsticks.

RATTLER
Materials
- a round salt carton
- tape
- some dry beans, rice, or pebbles

Pour some beans into the salt spout of your carton. Close the spout and seal it with tape.

Then make a small hole in the center of each end of the salt carton. Push a stick that is as long as two salt cartons through both holes. Put tape at the places where the stick goes through to hold it tightly. Add a tassel.

You can decorate it with crayons.

People in orchestras call rattlers like these "maracas."

SWISH
SWISH
SWISH

SANDPAPER BLOCKS
Materials
- 2 easy-to-hold building blocks
- scissors
- coarse sandpaper
- thumbtacks or glue

Cut two pieces of sandpaper, each a little larger than the side of a block. Thumbtack pieces of sandpaper to blocks, or paste in place.

Rub, rub . . . swish, swish.

build
a secret
hideaway

Here are some ways you can make a secret hideaway at home.

You can make one in an unused corner of your basement, garage, attic, or game room. Every corner has two walls. Build a third wall and you have a hideaway.

a crepe-paper wall

Hammer a nail in each of the corner walls, as high up as you want the crepe-paper wall to be. Tie a string from one nail to the other. Hang crepe-paper strips from the string to the floor. You can fasten them at the bottom with another string stretched between the walls. Be sure to leave one or two strips loose at the bottom so that you have a door.

a carton hideaway

A cardboard carton, large enough to walk into, makes a good hideaway. Turn it so that the box opens on its side. Let one of the flaps be the door. Tape the other one closed.

a folding-screen wall

If you don't have an old folding screen to use, make your own. Find several large cardboard boxes. Cut the boxes open and spread them flat. Tape them together, and refold them into a zigzag screen.

a table hideaway

A table turned on its side makes a good hideaway. Cover it with an old sheet or blanket.

Other secret corners can be made in the basement or attic with wood planks or insulation-board scraps.

When you have made your hideaway, think of some password. Then, don't let anyone in unless they first give you the password.

PARADE SOLDIERS

Materials

- an empty toilet paper roll for each soldier
- a pipe cleaner for the arms
- crayons or poster paints
- something like a nail to make armholes

Color or paint a soldier's face, a hat, and a parade uniform on each paper roll. See Picture.

Punch holes for the arms on each side of the roll. The holes should be made at the line where the soldier's head and uniform meet. Push a pipe cleaner through the holes.

Bend the pipe cleaner arms to make elbows and hands.

You can put a toothpick rifle in your soldier's hand, or give him a paper flag.

Here Comes The Band!

You can make a military band out of your soldiers. Just give them musical instruments to hold.

Out of these

cottage cheese carton	paper clip	paper circles	toothpick and clay

Make these

bass drum	trombone	cymbals	baton

A PIPE-CLEANER FAMILY

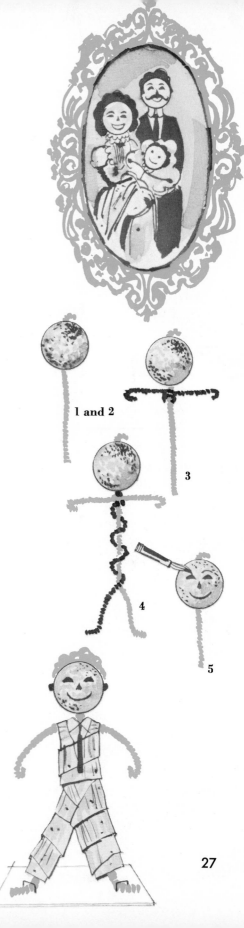

Materials

• a round cork bead or a small round cork for the head • 3 pipe cleaners for the body • crepe paper for clothes • scissors • paste or glue • paints • yarn and string • a piece of cardboard

1. Push one end of a pipe cleaner through the hole in a cork bead. If it does not go through easily, make the hole bigger by twisting a nail in it.

2. Bend the top of the pipe cleaner to keep it from slipping through the cork.

3. Twist another pipe cleaner just below the cork so that it holds the head in place. It will make the arms.

4. Start wrapping another pipe cleaner around the body just under the arms. This pipe cleaner will become one of the doll's legs. Bend the end of each leg for a foot.

5. Paint a face on the cork. You can add hair by pasting on some yarn or string. To make clothes, twist crepe-paper strips around the pipe-cleaner body.

The people will stand up if you paste or staple the feet to a piece of cardboard. You can also make them sit or lie down.

1 and 2

3

4

5

27

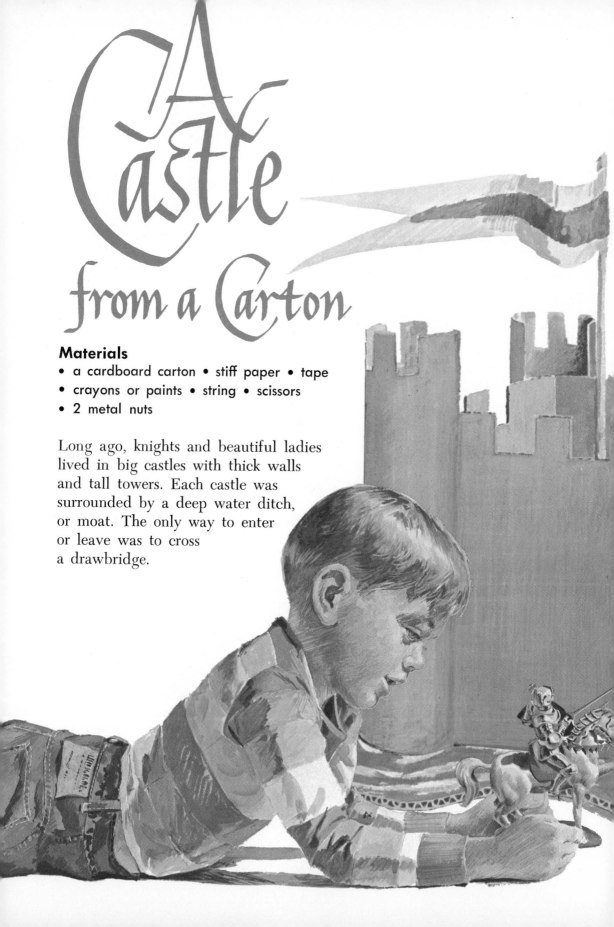

A Castle from a Carton

Materials
- a cardboard carton • stiff paper • tape
- crayons or paints • string • scissors
- 2 metal nuts

Long ago, knights and beautiful ladies lived in big castles with thick walls and tall towers. Each castle was surrounded by a deep water ditch, or moat. The only way to enter or leave was to cross a drawbridge.

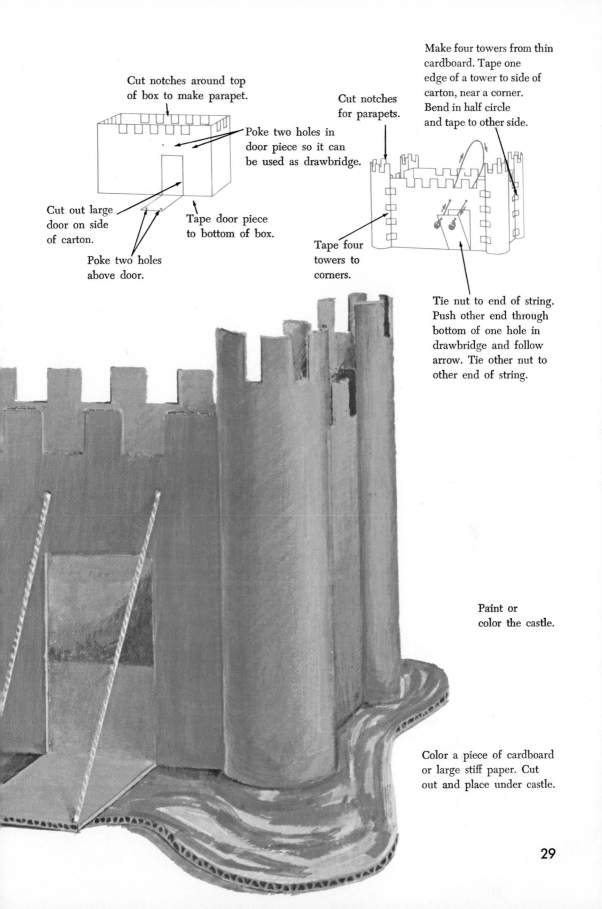

Cut notches around top
of box to make parapet.

Cut notches
for parapets.

Make four towers from thin
cardboard. Tape one
edge of a tower to side of
carton, near a corner.
Bend in half circle
and tape to other side.

Poke two holes in
door piece so it can
be used as drawbridge.

Cut out large
door on side
of carton.

Tape door piece
to bottom of box.

Poke two holes
above door.

Tape four
towers to
corners.

Tie nut to end of string.
Push other end through
bottom of one hole in
drawbridge and follow
arrow. Tie other nut to
other end of string.

Paint or
color the castle.

Color a piece of cardboard
or large stiff paper. Cut
out and place under castle.

29

an add-a-room
HOUSE

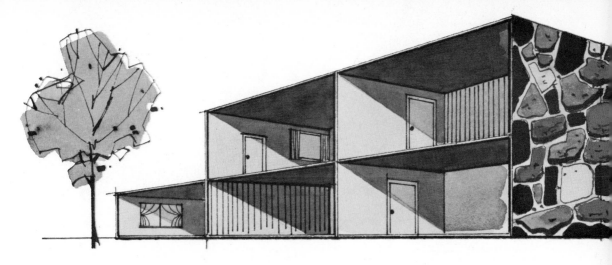

Materials

- 5 cardboard cartons, all the same size
- thin cardboard or stiff paper
- tempera or poster paint • tape • thumbtacks

You can change the style of this Add-a-Room House whenever you wish.

1. Cut out the top from each carton.

2. Cover the rough edges with tape.

3. Arrange the cartons to form the kind of building you want. Arrange them one way to make a town house with a two-car garage. Pile them up to make a skyscraper. Spread them out to make a rambling ranch house. If the cartons slip out of place, you can tack pieces of cardboard over the seams.

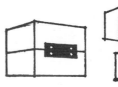

How To Make Windows and Doors

4. Draw windows and doors on separate pieces of thin cardboard or stiff paper. The windows and doors can be any size you wish. They can be plain or fancy.

5. Cut out the windows and doors.

6. Trace around the cutout windows and doors on other pieces of stiff paper to make a second set exactly like the first.

7. Decide where you wish to have a door on your house. Pick up a pair of doors that are exactly alike. Put one of them inside the box, and the other one directly behind it on the outside of the box. Push one or two thumbtacks through the box to hold the door in place.

8. Do the same with the other windows and doors.
The windows and doors can be moved if you wish.

FURNITURE

a pudding box

a television set

cardboard and spool

a coffee table

from these odds and ends you can

a frozen-food box

a fireplace

a kitchen-match box

a couch

small matchboxes

a chest of drawers

for the house you build

a stove

a washer

a sink

an end table

a chair

a dressing table

make all this furniture

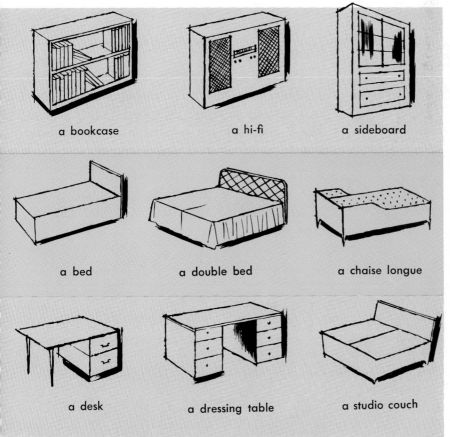

a bookcase

a hi-fi

a sideboard

a bed

a double bed

a chaise longue

a desk

a dressing table

a studio couch

Use an oval powder box for a dining-room table or bath tub.

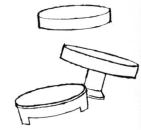

Turn paper handkerchiefs into curtains, bedspreads, or tablecloths.

Fold corrugated paper to have a folding screen or patio chair.

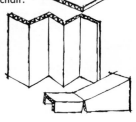

Paste bits of paper on pipe cleaners to have lamps, coat trees, and little green plants.

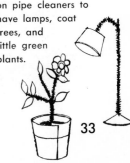

33

How To Make a
Submarine

Materials
- 4 cardboard cartons—3 the same size and one large enough to sit in
- pencil
- blunt scissors
- tape
- a large piece of heavy paper like wrapping paper or a paper cleaning-bag

Here's how you do it:

1. Place the large carton on end. Number it 3. This will be the conning tower. Place two cartons in front. Number them 1 and 2. Place the last carton behind the conning tower. Number it 4. See Pictures.

2. Tape down the flaps and any loose ends of Cartons 1, 2, and 3. Several small pieces of any kind of tape will do fine. Do not tape down Carton 4.

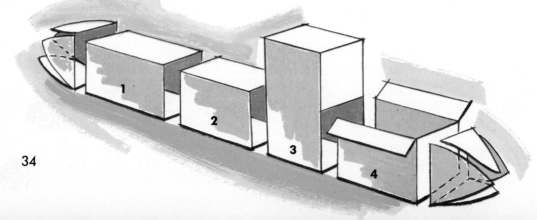

3. To make a doorway into the conning tower, push Carton 4 against Carton 3. Draw a line where the top of 4 comes. That's how high the doorway should be. Saw out or cut out the part of Carton 3 below this line. Save this cardboard.

4. To make a hatch, or door, open top flaps of Carton 4.

5. To make a passageway into the conning tower, cut out the end of Carton 4, next to Carton 3. Save this cardboard. See Picture.

6. You now have a submarine. If you want to make it more streamlined like a real submarine, you can add a cigar-shaped bow and stern. See the steps below.

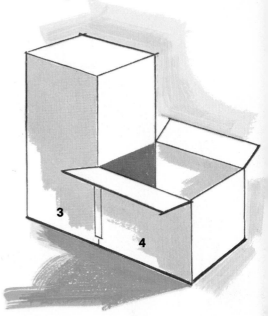

How To Make a Nose and Tail

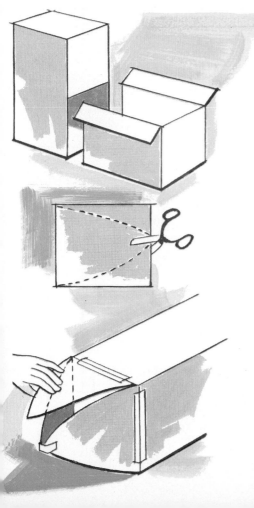

7. Cut out the ends of Cartons 1 and 2 where they come together. These two cardboard pieces together with the cardboard you cut out to make the passageway into the conning tower, will make a bow and stern.

8. Draw a cigar-shaped pattern on one piece of cardboard. Cut it out. See Picture.

9. Trace around this pattern on the other three pieces of cardboard. Cut them out.

10. Tape two pieces to the front for a bow. Tape points together.

11. Tape the other two pieces to Carton 4 for the stern. Tape points together.

12. Cut pieces of heavy paper to cover the empty spaces at the bow and the stern. Tape the pieces of paper to the cardboard.

Tape all the cartons together, and you've built your submarine. The next page will tell you how to install a real periscope in the conning tower.

How To Make a Real
Periscope

Materials

- long wax-paper or a foil-paper box
- a small piece of paper
- a piece of tablet back or thin cardboard
- tape, any kind will do
- scissors
- 2 small pocket mirrors

1. You will need to know which end of your long box is the top. So mark a "T" for "top" at one end.

2. To make an important pattern that you will need, trace a square exactly the same size as the end of the box on a piece of paper. Cut out the square. Fold the square to make a triangle. See Picture.

3. Stand box up with the "T" at the top. Place your triangle pattern along the bottom edge of the box, folded edge slanting upward. See Picture.

4. Draw a line on the box along the slant. Cut a slit on this line.

5. Around the corner from the top end of the slit, cut a window big enough to look through. See Picture.

6. Place the triangle pattern at the top of the box, on the same side as the lower slit, folded side slanting down. See Picture. Draw a line along the slant. Cut a slit on this line.

7. Around the corner from the top slit draw and cut out a top window. This window must be on the opposite side of the box from the bottom window.

8. You will need mounts for your mirrors. Draw and cut out two pieces of cardboard as wide as the box and a little longer than the slant of your triangle pattern. Glue one mirror to each mount. See Picture.

9. Slide one mirror in the lower slit, looking-side up. Slide the other mirror in the top slit, looking-side down.

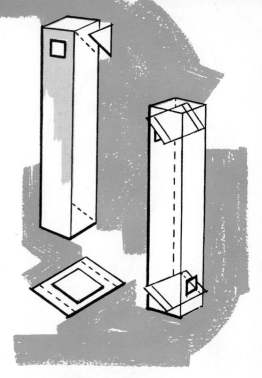

To Use Your Periscope in the Submarine

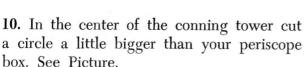

10. In the center of the conning tower cut a circle a little bigger than your periscope box. See Picture.

11. To make a periscope mount, take a piece of heavy cardboard. Cut a circle a little bigger than the one in the conning tower.

12. Set the periscope box on this circle and draw around the square box. Cut out.

13. Remove one mirror and slip the periscope into this circle mount. Replace mirror.

14. Put one end of the periscope through the hole in the conning tower, so that the mount is outside the box.

You can add all kinds of finishing touches. You can make a control panel on the inside of the conning tower. You can add an anchor, and even paint on a name.

funny face masks

Materials
- a paper plate
- string
- crayons
- a paper bag
- a piece of cardboard

Draw a face on a paper plate. Cut out the eyeholes and color the face.

Punch a small hole on each side of the face near the edge of the plate. These two holes should be a little higher than the eyeholes.

Tie a piece of string from one hole to the other. The string will go around the back of your head to hold the mask in front of your face.

Instead of a paper plate, you can use a piece of thin cardboard, or a large paper bag.

Add hair by gluing bits of yarn to the top of your mask.

Look in the mirror—

BOO!

pictures! pictures! pictures!

Did you ever paint a picture with a toothbrush, or an old sponge, or colored soapsuds? On the next pages you will find ways to use almost anything to make pretty and unusual pictures.

HOW TO GET THE COLOR YOU WANT

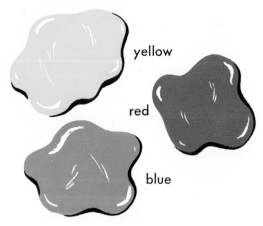

yellow

red

blue

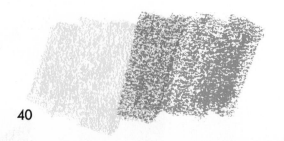

When you paint with tempera, you can use the colors that are in the jars. Or you can mix those colors to make new colors.

With only three colors—red, blue, and yellow—you can make any color you want.

When you want to mix colors to make new colors, try doing it first to be sure you are making the color you want. Mix them on a plate or on a try-out piece of paper.

You can also mix colors when you color with chalk or crayon. Just put one color on top of another color.

The chart on page 41 tells you what color you will get when you mix two colors together.

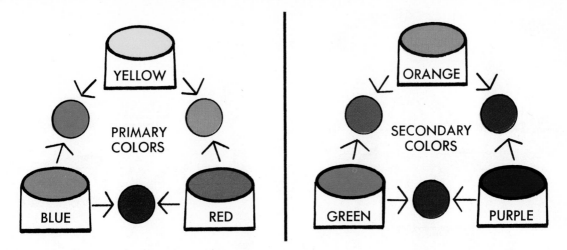

What the New Color Will Be

Red, blue, and yellow are called the primary colors. You can mix them to make all the other colors.

The colors you make from the three primary ones can be mixed to make still other colors. The chart also shows what colors you can make from them.

Make the Color Light or Dark

Add water to tempera or poster paints to make a thinner color.

With other paints, chalk, or crayons, add a little white to make a lighter color. To make a darker color, add a little black.

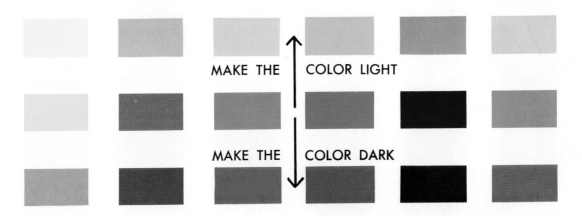

MAKE THE | COLOR LIGHT

MAKE THE | COLOR DARK

CHALK PICTURES

Here are two different ways to make chalk pictures.

Dry Chalk

Put one chalk color on top of another. Then rub the chalk with your finger to blend the colors together. You'll probably find that the colors you get are very soft and delicate-looking.

CHALK WITH WATER

You can make bold, bright
pictures with chalk, too.
First wet the paper. Let the
extra water drip off the page.
Then draw on the wet
paper with the colored chalk. Be
sure to spread newspapers on
your work space before you
start painting with chalk in this
way, for it can be messy.

How To Keep Chalk Pictures from Smearing

A good way to take care of the
chalk pictures you
want to keep is to
spray them with a special
fluid called "fixative."
You can get fixative
at almost any
art supply store.
Fixative becomes
a film over the chalk
and keeps it from smearing.

43

FINGER PAINTING

With special finger paints, you can paint pictures with your fingers and hands instead of with a brush.

GETTING READY

Finger paints are sold at art supply stores, stationery stores, variety stores, or dime stores. Or you can make your own finger paints by mixing starch and poster paint. Ask your mother to boil some laundry starch for you. Let it cool. Pour it into several jars, and mix a little poster paint with the starch—a different color in each jar.

Finger painting is fun, but it can be messy, too. So before you start finger painting, put on a smock or apron, and cover the table or floor with newspapers where you plan to work.

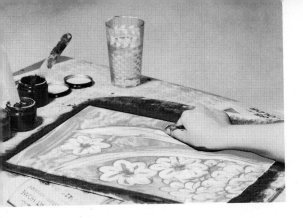

HOW TO FINGER-PAINT

Shiny shelf paper is the best kind to finger-paint on.

Wet the paper in a pan of water or under a water faucet. Spread it out smoothly on the newspapers. If the paper gets too dry before you finish painting, sprinkle some more water on it.

Spoon some paint from the jar and put it on the paper.

Use your thumb and fingers for most of your picture. But also use the side of your hand and arm for big, sweeping strokes. Use your finger tips and nails to make fine details.

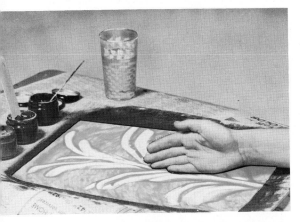

When your picture is finished, let it dry. Ask your mother to help you press it with a warm iron to smooth out any wrinkles in the paper. Finger-paint designs make beautiful wrapping paper for gifts.

You can also finger-paint on things made of glass and plastic. If you do, put shellac over your picture to protect it.

SOAPSUDS PICTURES

Materials
- ½ cup of dry detergent, or a capful of liquid detergent
- 2 tablespoons of liquid starch
- brown wrapping paper
- poster paints or food coloring
- an egg beater • a mixing bowl
- an old newspaper • a spoon

Beat the detergent and the liquid starch with an egg beater in a mixing bowl. When it is like thick marshmallow frosting, you have beaten it enough. Now you have enough soapsuds for painting three or four pictures.

If you want soapsuds of several different colors, put the mixture into different jars. Then add just a few drops of color to the different jars and stir.

Put down a newspaper to work on.

Dip the colored soapsuds from the jar with your fingers and paint on some brown wrapping paper.

If you want a darker color, add more coloring until you get the shade you want.

Paint on with fingers

If the soapsuds thicken too much to paint with easily, add a little more starch when you are painting and beat it into the mixture with a spoon.

When you have finished your picture, let it dry lying flat on the newspaper before you show it.

Add starch if mixture thickens

47

Paint with ANYTHING

You can paint pictures with almost anything that puts marks on paper.

Using a Paintbrush

Keep a jar of water handy when you paint with poster paints, tempera, or water colors. You can clean the brush in the water when you change from one color to the next.

You can also use the water to make the color lighter. The more water you have on your brush, the thinner the color will be.

Using an Old Toothbrush

Toothbrush bristles are stiffer than paintbrush bristles. So the pictures you paint with a toothbrush will show the brush strokes clearly.

Use Different Kinds of Paper

Rough paper or bumpy paper will make your paintings look different. Try painting on a rough paper towel, or on the ripply side of a cardboard carton, or on the scratchy side of an old piece of sandpaper.

48

Using a Sponge

You can paint pictures with a sponge. Dip it in wet paint and touch it to the paper lightly. Notice that sponge marks look different from paintbrush marks. Now try pressing the sponge down hard. Then try rubbing it on the paper. Then try twisting the sponge as you press down on it.

Using an Old Rag

You can paint with a rag made of burlap or towel cloth just the way you paint with a sponge. But the marks of the rag will be different from those of a sponge.

For the most fun of all, try out all these ways of painting on one picture.

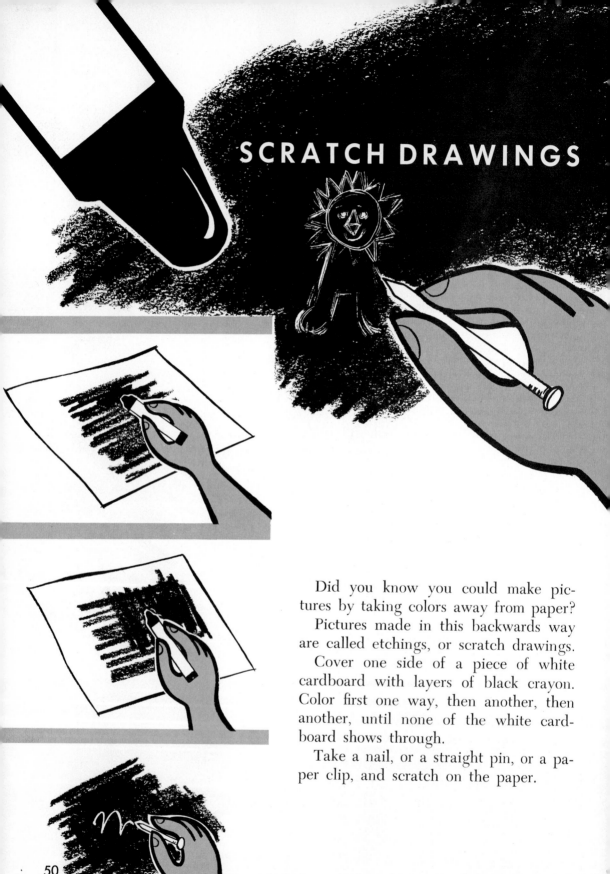

SCRATCH DRAWINGS

Did you know you could make pictures by taking colors away from paper?

Pictures made in this backwards way are called etchings, or scratch drawings.

Cover one side of a piece of white cardboard with layers of black crayon. Color first one way, then another, then another, until none of the white cardboard shows through.

Take a nail, or a straight pin, or a paper clip, and scratch on the paper.

Scratch out the main outline of your picture first. Then make parts of the picture stand out with little scratches put close together. Try wavy lines, wiggly lines, zigzag lines, wide lines, and tiny lines.

TRY OTHER COLORS

Try other colors over different kinds of colored paper.

SPATTER A PICTURE

Materials
• an old toothbrush • a saucer • a tree leaf • a sheet of paper • poster paints or ink • a piece of screen or a flat stick

GETTING READY

Put old newspapers over the table where you plan to work, so that the paint won't spatter on the table. Put on an apron or a smock.

Pour some poster paint or ink into a saucer. If you use poster paint, add water to it to make it thinner.

MAKING SPATTER PICTURES

Place a leaf on the paper.

Dip your toothbrush in the saucer of paint.

Hold your screen over the paper and brush it. Paint will spatter on the paper except where the leaf is covering it. A screen with big holes will make big spatter spots. Small holes will make small spatter spots.

If you use an ice-cream stick instead of a screen, rub your toothbrush against the ice-cream stick to make the paint spatter.

After you have covered the paper with spatters, pick up the leaf.

You can use the same leaf again and again on other sheets of paper. Or you can use any shapes you want like cutouts, flowers, and coins.

53

PICTURES MADE OF BUMPY DOUGH

Materials

- ¾ cup of flour
- ¼ cup of salt
- water
- tempera paints
- several containers, one for each color of dough
- a mixing bowl
- a spoon
- cardboard or heavy paper

How To Make The Dough Paint

Mix salt and flour with a few spoonfuls of water. Keep adding water, a spoonful at a time, until the mixture is as soft as the dough your mother uses for cookies.

When the dough is just right, put some in each of your containers. Then add a spoonful of tempera to each container, and mix it in with the dough.

How To Make a Dough Picture

Now you can start building your picture on your pieces of cardboard. Shape each part of the picture with your fingers before you stick it to the cardboard.

You can use brown dough for a tree trunk. Use green for leaves. Add extra dough where you want the bumps in your picture to stand up more. If you wish, you can put seeds, yarn, or other odds and ends into the dough as part of the picture. Let the dough dry.

FUNNY SPLASH DESIGNS

Materials
- 2 pieces of white paper
- tempera or poster paint
- a rolling pin

Splash some paint of different colors on one sheet of paper. Put another piece of paper on top of it. Roll the paper with a rolling pin. Lift up the top piece of paper to see what kind of picture you have!

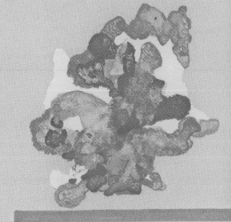

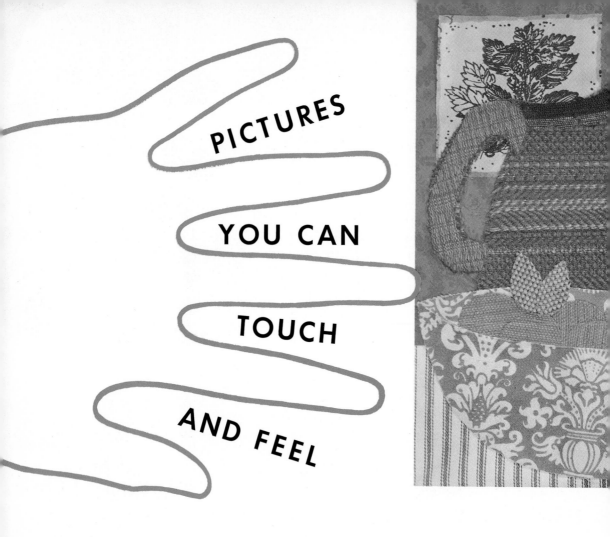

PICTURES YOU CAN TOUCH AND FEEL

You can make pictures out of things that are smooth, slippery, knobby, prickly, hard, soft, tickly, scratchy, bumpy, or ripply.

Or you can make a picture out of many different pieces of the same kind of thing, like bits of yarn or pieces of cloth.

These pictures that are fun to touch and fun to see are called "collages."

You can collect the pieces for your collage anywhere—in the woods, at the edge of a river, or even in a junk yard.

One collage could be made of nuts and bark and twigs and leaves and pieces of grass. Another could be made of cotton, buttons, lace, and ribbon.

Whatever things you choose, put them on a big sheet of paper. Move them around until they make the kind of picture you like best. Now paste, or staple, or tape them to the paper. Hang your collage on the wall.

SHADOW PICTURES

Materials

- white paper
- colored paper
- a flashlight or reading lamp
- blunt scissors
- a thumbtack
- a pencil
- paste

Tack a sheet of white paper on the wall.

Have a friend sit in front of the paper. The shadow of his head should fall on the paper when you shine a light on him.

Draw a pencil line around the shadow.

Take the paper off the wall and cut along the line.

Paste the shadow picture on colored paper so that it stands out clearly.

You can make a scrapbook with shadow pictures of all your friends.

PICTURES
made from
PAPER

Tear up lots of pieces of different kinds of paper—newspapers, colored drawing paper, paper bags, and notebook paper. The pieces can be of any size.

Put the pieces of paper on a large sheet of plain paper. Move them around until they make the kind of picture you want. Paste them in place.

If you wish, you can add lines with crayon, paint, or colored yarn.

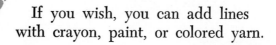

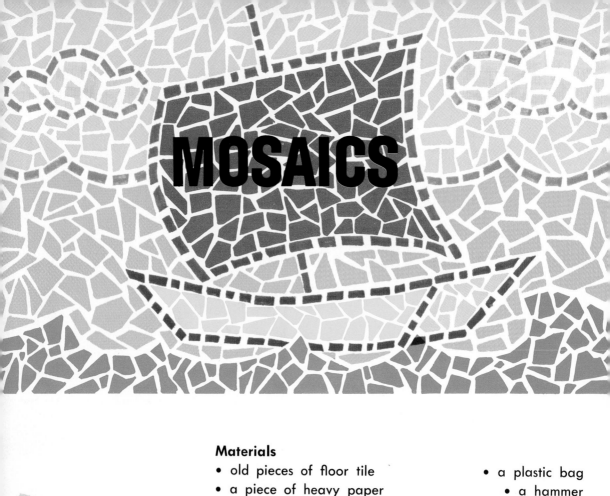

MOSAICS

Materials
- old pieces of floor tile
- a piece of heavy paper
- plaster of Paris
- a plastic bag
- a hammer
- blunt scissors
- glue

Pictures made of pieces of colored stone, glass, or tile are called "mosaics." You can make one with broken tiles. Ask the salesman at a floor-covering store for any unwanted floor tiles of the kind that will break. He will probably give you some.

Put several tiles in a plastic bag. Hammer the bag to break the tiles into pieces.

Draw a picture on heavy paper. Arrange the broken tile pieces on your drawing so that they make the same picture. Use tiles of different colors for different parts of your picture.

60

When you have arranged the pieces the way you want them, glue each one to the paper. The easiest way is to glue only a part of the picture at a time. Cover a part with glue and stick the tile pieces down. You can move the pieces around in the wet glue to get them in the right place.

After the glue is dry, mix some plaster of Paris and pour it into the cracks between the pieces. You can push and mold the plaster of Paris into the holes and cracks. Let it dry for a day. Then cut off the extra paper.

Tile mosaics can be used for hot plates, tray decorations, or pictures for the wall.

If you have enough tile pieces, you can decorate a whole table top with them.

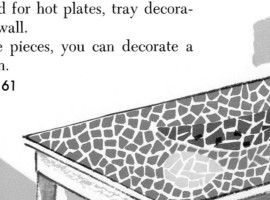

How to draw a FUNNY

draw
light
guide
lines

It's easy to draw a funny face —start with the shape of a circle or an oval.

Then draw two light lines, one through the middle from the top to the bottom, the other through the middle from side to side.

EARS
FRONT VIEW

SIDE VIEW

NOSES
FRONT VIEW

SIDE VIEW

flat oval

long oval

FACE

Here are some ideas you can use for your funny face

triangle

square

circle

Now put a nose on the up-and-down line, and some ears on the ends of the side-to-side line. Then draw two eyes on the side-to-side line, and eyebrows a little above the eyes. Then put a mouth a little below the nose. Add some hair or a moustache or glasses and a pipe.

63

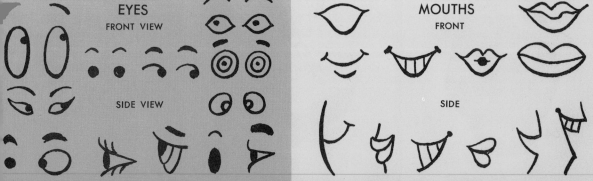

EYES
FRONT VIEW

SIDE VIEW

MOUTHS
FRONT

SIDE

Printing
with
Potatoes

Materials
- a large potato
- a paring knife
- paper
- poster paints

Cut a potato in half.

Mark a square, a circle, a diamond, an "x", or some other simple picture on the flat side of one of the halves. If you draw a letter of the alphabet, make it backward so that it will print right.

Cut away some of the potato inside your design. See Picture. Now when you put paint on the potato, only the flat edge around the design will print.

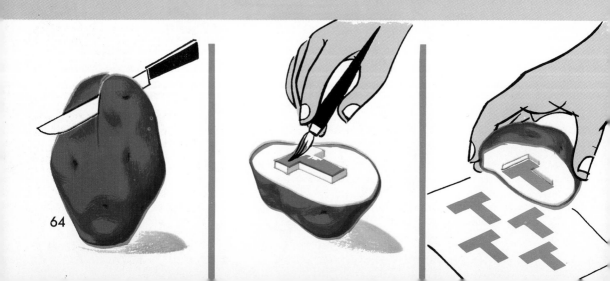

Print Simple Shapes First

Cover the flat side of the potato with poster paint. Push it against the paper to make it print.

You can print the picture as many times as you wish, if you cover the potato with paint before each printing.

Another kind of potato printer can be made by leaving the picture flat and cutting away everything but the picture. Now when you put paint on the potato, only the picture will print.

You can use each half of the potato for a different kind of potato printer.

Try printing with different-sized corks, spools, bottle caps, erasers, and other things.

Print with Other Things

PRINTING WITH
TIN CANS

Materials

- a tin can
- tempera or poster paint
- rope
- a pie tin or a deep plate
- glue
- tape
- paper

Out of a tin can you can make a roller that prints. It will make fine designs on paper for gift wrapping.

Cover the jagged edge at the open end of the can with tape to protect yourself from cuts.

Twist rope around the can and glue it in place. See Picture. You might wish to cut the rope into a number of pieces and glue each one to the can. You can twist each piece to whatever shape you wish before you glue it in place.

Make sure that the glue is dry before you begin printing with the can roller.

Put some tempera or poster paint in the pie tin. Roll the can in the paint. The paint will stick to the rope, but not to the can.

Now roll the can over a sheet of paper, and the rope will print the shapes. Roll the can in the paint each time before you roll it over the paper. You can print the design as many times as you wish.

Try making other designs with felt or wool cut-outs.

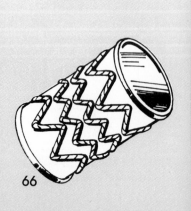

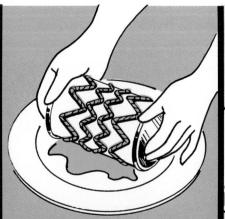

squeezing and shaping

Take a soggy ball of paper, some flour and water dough, or some modeling clay. Punch it and squeeze it. And soon you can have a rabbit, a tiny man, or many other shapes. On the next pages are ways to model.

How To Mold a Penguin

BEGIN WITH A BALL

Materials
- modeling clay
- a pointed stick or a pencil

To make a penguin:

Roll a large round ball of clay for the body.

Roll three small balls, all the same size, for the head and the wings.

Stick the head on top of the body.

Flatten the other two balls until they are shaped like the two wings in the picture. Stick the wings on the body.

Roll two smaller balls for the feet, and flatten them. Stick them in place.

A tiny ball can be pointed to make a beak. Stick it in the middle of the face.

Smooth the clay where the pieces are stuck to each other so that the lines where they join do not show.

Use a pointed stick to make dents for the eyes.

HOW TO MOLD

To make an elephant:

Roll two big balls, one for the body and the other for the trunk and the legs.

Roll three smaller balls, all the same size, for the head and the two ears. Flatten the two balls for the ears, and stick them on the head. Stick head to body.

Roll the ball for the trunk and the legs into a sausage shape. Break four short

BEGIN WITH A ROLL

How To Mold a Sausage Dog

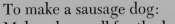

To make a sausage dog:

Make a long roll for the body.

Make a ball for the head and four small rolls for the legs. Stick them on the body.

A tiny roll can be the tail and a smaller one can be the nose. Two flattened balls can be the ears.

Mark the nose, eyes, and mouth with the pointed stick.

AN ELEPHANT

pieces from this for the legs. Stick them on the body. The rest of the sausage shape is the trunk. Stick it on the head.

Smooth the clay where the pieces are attached to each other.

Two tiny balls can be rolled out to make tusks. Mark the eyes with a pointed stick.

69

MOLD A CLAY HEAD

Materials

- modeling clay
- a pointed stick or a pencil

THE HEAD

Take a big lump of clay and knead it like dough to get rid of any air holes or soft spots. Roll it into a ball for the head.

Roll a smaller ball of clay for the neck. Stick it to the head. Smooth the clay where the two balls are stuck together so that the line between them does not show. Flatten the bottom of the neck so that the head will stand.

THE FACE

The corners of the mouth and the eyes turn up on a happy face and down on a sad face. Big, round eyes give any face a look of surprise.

Draw a faint line around the head, halfway down from the top of it. On this line mark the two eyes with the pointed stick.

Shape a lump of clay for the nose and add it to the face, between the eyes and just below the line.

70

Two ears can be shaped out of other pieces of clay. Place them on the sides of the head just below the line. Smooth the clay after you stick on the ears and the nose.

Roll out a worm-shaped piece of clay, and cut pieces off for the eyebrows and the lips.

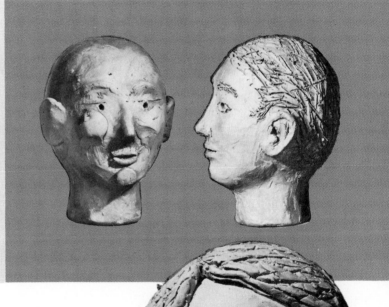

Add extra clay to the face to build up the chin and the cheeks. Make hair marks with a pointed stick. Add pieces and lumps of clay to make more hair for the heads of girls.

How To Make Clay People

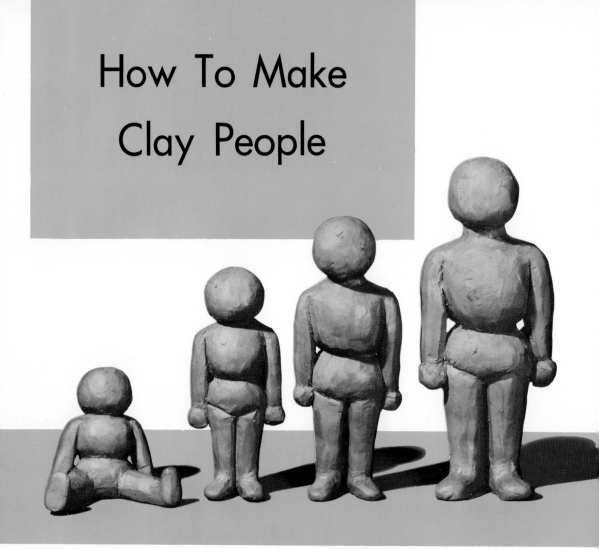

Materials
- modeling clay
- a pointed stick or a pencil

Clay people of different sizes are made of pieces of clay that are shaped into balls and rolls.

The bodies of grown-up people are longer and thinner than those of babies and small children, and the shoulders of grownups are wider. Grownups also have longer arms and legs.

The pictures on this page show how many balls and sausage-shaped pieces of clay are needed for the different kinds of bodies.

Squeeze and mash the clay before you roll it into balls and sausage-shaped pieces so that you get rid of any air holes and soft spots.

Stick the balls and sausage-shaped pieces together to make a body. Smooth the clay where the pieces join.

Use the pointed stick and bits of clay to shape the parts of the face and to mark the lines for clothes.

The clay person can be standing, sitting, lying down, or crawling. You may have to lean him against another piece of clay or a stick if he is standing.

A CLAY BOWL

Materials

- hardening clay
- liquid detergent
- an old sheet or a piece of cloth
- tempera paint
- shellac

1. Lay cloth on table or floor. Put a large lump of clay on it. Squeeze and mash the clay to get rid of air holes and soft spots, and roll it into a ball.

2. Punch a hole in the center of the ball.

Use your fingers to make the hole larger and larger until the clay is shaped like a bowl.

Painting the

Now you are ready to paint the bowl. Mix tempera with about a spoonful of liquid detergent. Clay is oily, and the detergent helps the paint to stick to the bowl. If the paint does not stick well, add more detergent.

When the paint is dry, cover the bowl with shellac to protect the paint.

3. Work your fingers out and up to make the sides of the bowl thinner.

When the bowl is shaped as you want it, smooth the inside and the outside.

4. You can stick a thin roll of clay to the outside of the bowl for a handle.

Bowl

A CLAY BOWL
MADE WITH ROLLS

- hardening clay
- detergent
- a saucer or a cardboard circle
- tempera paint
- an old sheet or a piece of cloth
- shellac

Lay cloth on a table or on the floor.

Flatten a big lump of clay. Put a saucer or a cardboard circle on top of the flat clay. Cut away the clay around the edge of the saucer. See Picture. The circle of clay that is left will be the bottom of the bowl.

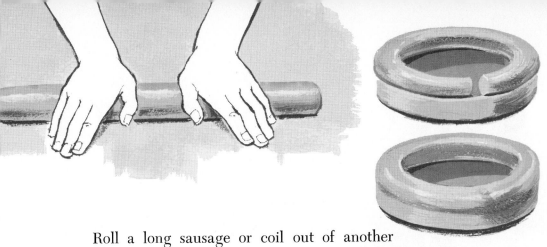

Roll a long sausage or coil out of another ball of clay. Bend it around the edge of the circle of clay. See Picture. Smooth the pieces together.

Roll another coil in the same way and stick it on top of the first coil. Then add another and another. Smooth the pieces together as you make the sides of the bowl taller.

LONGER COIL

SHORTER COIL

The top of the bowl will be wider than the sides if you put on a longer coil. It will be narrower if you put on a shorter coil.

A coil can also be used for a handle on the side of the bowl.

Paint the bowl with a mixture of tempera and some detergent. When the paint is dry, cover it with shellac.

CLAY JEWELRY

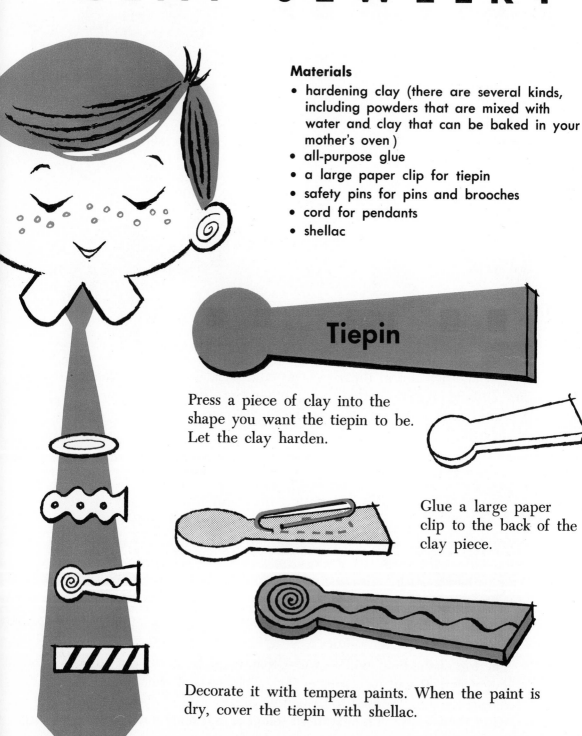

Materials
- hardening clay (there are several kinds, including powders that are mixed with water and clay that can be baked in your mother's oven)
- all-purpose glue
- a large paper clip for tiepin
- safety pins for pins and brooches
- cord for pendants
- shellac

Tiepin

Press a piece of clay into the shape you want the tiepin to be. Let the clay harden.

Glue a large paper clip to the back of the clay piece.

Decorate it with tempera paints. When the paint is dry, cover the tiepin with shellac.

Pins and Brooches

Press a piece of clay into the shape you want. Let it harden. If you wish, add a shiny pebble or a shell to the clay before it gets hard.

Glue a safety pin to the back of the clay. Paint the clay and let it dry before covering with shellac.

Pendants

Press a piece of clay into the shape you want. Before you let the clay harden, put a hole through it for the cord.

Paint the clay piece and put the cord through the hole. The cord must be long enough for the pendant to hang around your neck.

79

A CLAY ZOO

Do Not Feed THE ANIMALS

You can stick all sorts of odds and ends in clay to make funny animals.

You can add animal parts made of pipe cleaners, yarn, toothpicks, empty tooth-paste tubes, empty lipstick tubes, empty spools, cardboard, felt, or almost anything.

You can make a clay lion with two balls of clay—one for the body and one for the head. Make the neck out of a tooth-paste cap. Bits of pipe cleaner or yarn can be used for the tail and the lion's mane. Toothpicks or spools make good legs.

THIS WAY TO GIRAFFE

For a long-necked giraffe, you will also need a clay head and a clay body. The neck can be a pencil. Pipe cleaners will do for the legs and tail. And pipe cleaner bits, paper, or toothpicks can be used for the horns.

A toothpick will hold the head to the body of a clay elephant. The trunk is made out of an empty tooth-paste tube or a pipe cleaner. Add ears made of cardboard or felt, and tusks and tail made of pipe cleaners or paper. Set the elephant's body on legs made of spools.

A toothpick will also hold the head to the body of a clay monkey. Bend pipe cleaners for the legs and the tail. The ears are made of cardboard or felt.

81

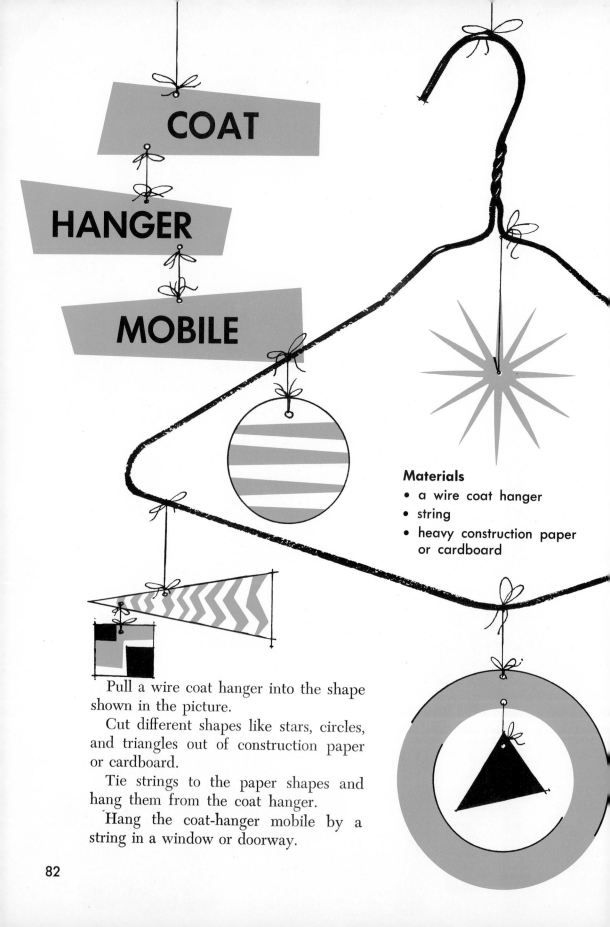

COAT
HANGER
MOBILE

Materials
- a wire coat hanger
- string
- heavy construction paper or cardboard

Pull a wire coat hanger into the shape shown in the picture.

Cut different shapes like stars, circles, and triangles out of construction paper or cardboard.

Tie strings to the paper shapes and hang them from the coat hanger.

Hang the coat-hanger mobile by a string in a window or doorway.

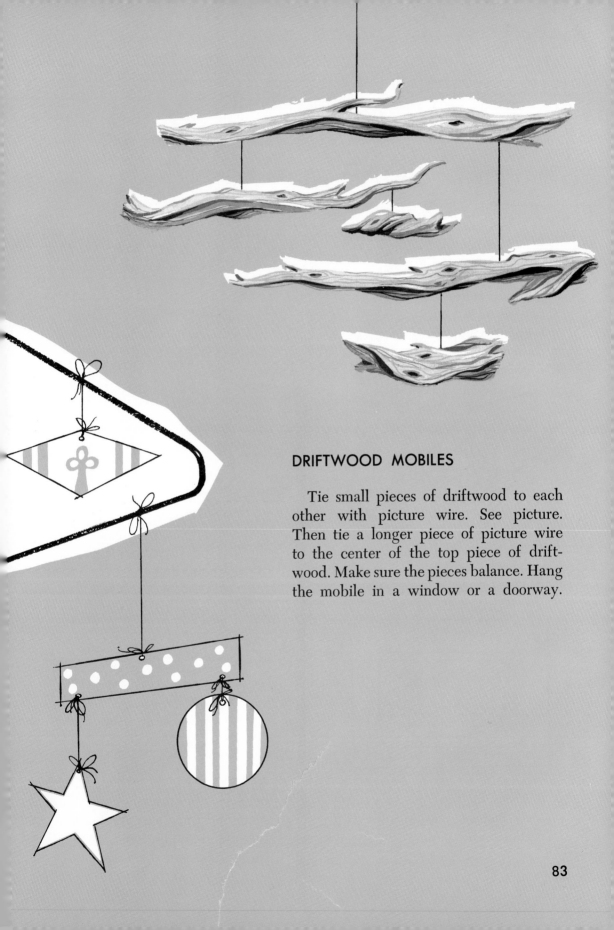

DRIFTWOOD MOBILES

Tie small pieces of driftwood to each other with picture wire. See picture. Then tie a longer piece of picture wire to the center of the top piece of driftwood. Make sure the pieces balance. Hang the mobile in a window or a doorway.

a turtle carved from SOAP

Materials
- a bar of soap
- a paring knife
- paper and a pencil
- tempera paints
- carbon paper
- a pointed stick

1. Scrape any lettering from the sides of a bar of soap.

2. Lay the soap on paper and trace around it.

3. Draw the top view of a turtle (see Picture) inside the soap outline on the paper.

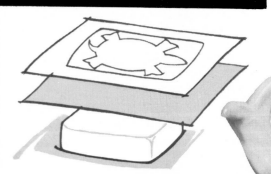

4. Put a piece of carbon paper between the drawing and the soap, and trace over the lines of the picture. This will make a carbon copy on the soap.

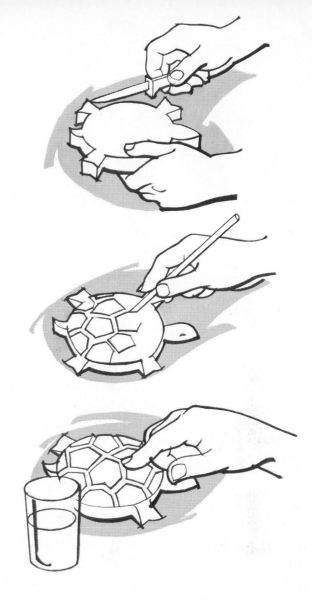

5. Bit by bit, cut away the outside edge of the soap until you reach the lines. When you carve, hold the knife edge away from your body. Don't try to cut away big chunks, just cut a little at a time.

6. Round out the top of the turtle's back with the knife. With a pointed stick you can make dents for the turtle's eyes and mark lines on its shell.

7. When you finish carving, smooth the sides by wetting the soap and rubbing it with your fingers.

Paint the turtle with tempera.

You can carve many other animals out of soap. Remember it is easier to carve the animals if you first draw a picture on the soap.

Try These

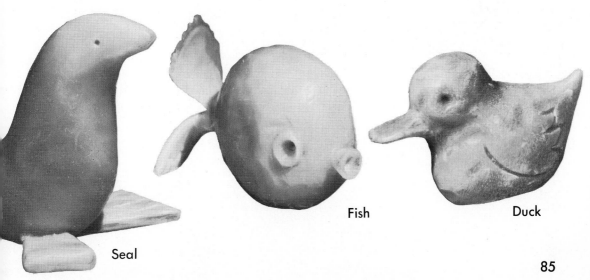

Seal

Fish

Duck

Doodle Bugs of Dough and Foil

Materials
- 2 cups of flour
- 1 cup of salt
- water (between $\frac{1}{2}$ and $\frac{3}{4}$ of a cup)
- a bowl
- 2 tablespoons of powdered alum (you can buy it in a drugstore)

- pipe cleaners
- glue
- tempera
- shellac
- tissue paper

Mix flour, salt, and alum in a bowl. Slowly mix in water. When the dough is thick and soft like modeling clay, it is ready to use.

Roll some of it into a ball, and shape it like the bug in the picture.

Cut up pipe cleaners for legs and feelers. Stick them into the sides of the dough bug.

Bend pipe cleaners into the shape of wings. See Picture. Glue tissue paper over the pipe cleaners. Stick the wings into the bug.

When the clay has dried for about a day, paint it with tempera paint. Cover the colors with shellac.

Try making birds, butterflies, and spiders in the same way.

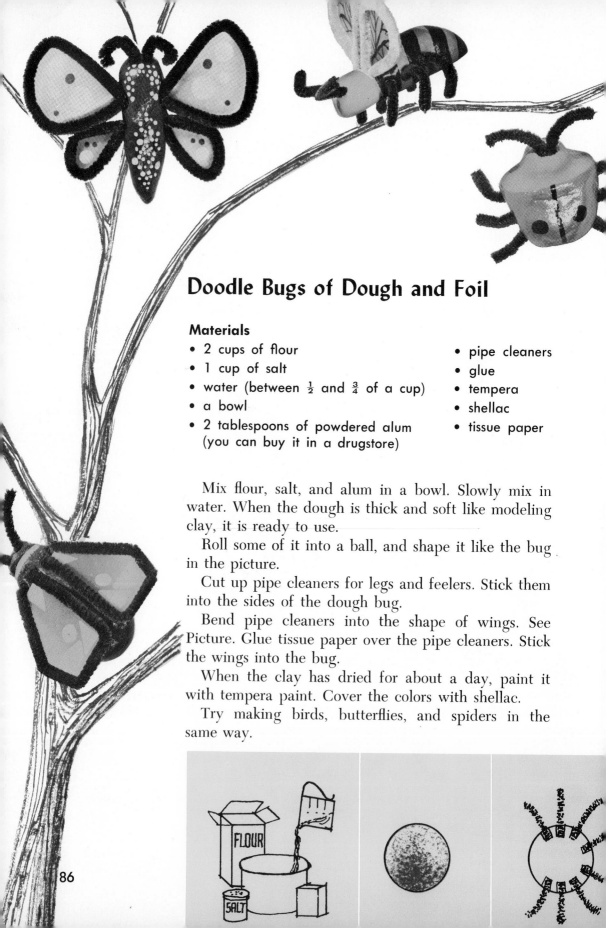

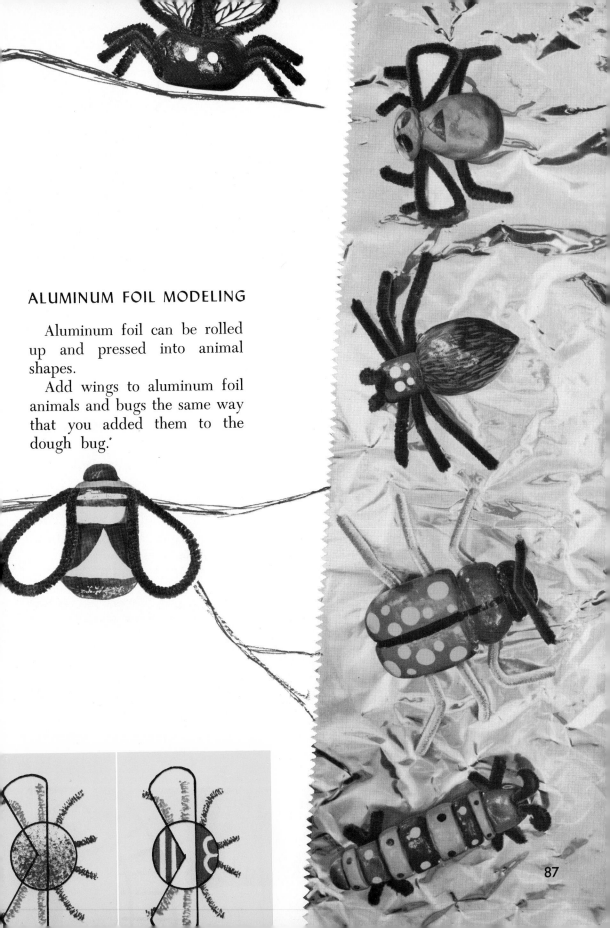

ALUMINUM FOIL MODELING

Aluminum foil can be rolled up and pressed into animal shapes.

Add wings to aluminum foil animals and bugs the same way that you added them to the dough bug.

Papier-Mâché

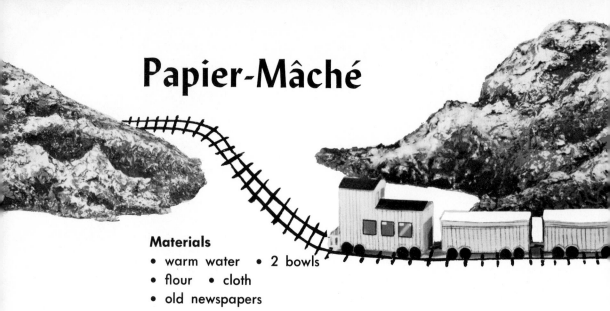

Materials
- warm water • 2 bowls
- flour • cloth
- old newspapers

PAPIER-MÂCHÉ PULP

You can squeeze and shape papier-mâché as if it were clay, when the paper is wet. When it dries, it becomes hard and strong.

Tear old newspapers or paper towels into tiny pieces, enough to nearly fill a bowl.

Put the paper bits in a bowl and pour warm water over them. Let them soak for more than an hour.

Scoop the wet paper into a piece of cloth. Hold the corners of the cloth together and twist to wring out all the water. Pour the water out of the bowl and put the damp paper back into it.

In a separate bowl mix two spoonfuls of flour with enough water to make a paste. Mix the paste with the damp paper.

A PAPIER-MÂCHÉ TOWN

With papier-mâché pulp, you can shape models of almost anything. Here's how to make a house, a tree, a tunnel, and a hill.

Houses are made by covering small milk or cream cartons with papier-mâché pulp. The peak at the top of each carton has the shape of a slanting roof. After the mâché is dry, you can paint the house and mark on the windows and the doors.

Trees are made of mâché wads stuck on top of lollipop sticks. Put another small wad of mâché at the bottom of the stick to give it a base to stand on. Paint the top wad green like the leaves of a tree and the bottom wad brown like the ground.

A tunnel is made from a bent piece of shirt cardboard covered with mâché. Cover a crumpled newspaper with mâché to make a hill. Paint it green or brown.

89

PAPIER-MÂCHÉ MASKS

1.

Make a Clay Face

Materials

- old newspapers • poster paints • clay
- oilcloth • shellac • flour • water

1. Lay a piece of oilcloth on your worktable. Put a large lump of clay on it. Shape the clay into a thick oval, larger around than your face. See Picture.

2. Add a nose, chin, ears, and lips with pieces of clay. Push dents in the clay for each eye.

Make a paste with flour and water. Put just enough flour into the water to make it look and feel like melted ice cream.

Tear old newspapers into strips, each about the size of a ruler.

3. Soak a few of the strips in plain water. Lay them across the clay face, this way and that way. Put on more strips, soaked in water, until the clay is all covered.

2.

Now dip the other strips into the paste, and lay them on top of the layer of wet strips.

When you have covered the wet paper with a layer of strips dipped in paste, put on another layer of strips dipped in paste, until you have six or more layers of paper over the clay.

Let the paper dry for a day and a night.

Dig out the clay.

4. Paint the face on the mask with poster paint. Then give it a coat of shellac.

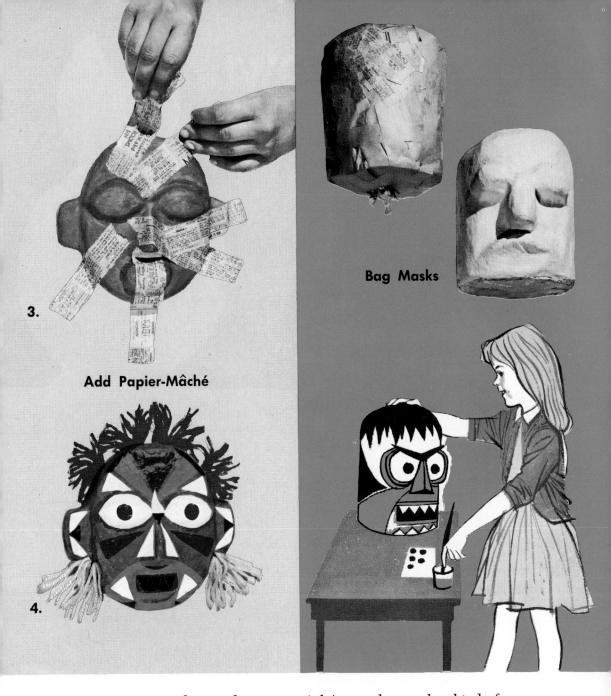

3.

Add Papier-Mâché

Bag Masks

4.

Cover a paper bag with papier-mâché to make another kind of mask that you can use as a decoration on a shelf or table.

Use a medium- or large-sized shopping bag. Crumple old newspapers and stuff them inside the bag. Put tape across the opening to keep the stuffing inside.

Now cover the bag with papier-mâché strips. Put lumps of papier-mâché in place for the nose, lips, and eyes. Cover these with more papier-mâché strips.

Let the mask dry. Paint it, cut open the bottom, and then pull the newspaper stuffing out of the bag.

91

ROLY-POLY OWL

Materials
- 2 round balloons • glue
- string • cardboard
- old newspapers • scissors
- flour • a pin
- water • poster paints

Blow up two round balloons, a large one for the body of your owl and a small one for the head. Tie a string to the end of each.

Mix enough flour with water to make a paste about as thick as melted ice cream.

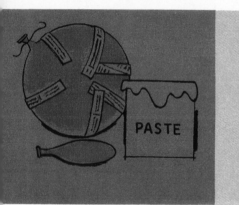 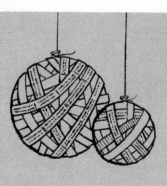 

Tear old newspapers into strips about the size of a ruler. Dip some of the strips in plain water. Cover one balloon by crisscrossing the wet strips over it. Leave the string uncovered.

After a balloon is completely covered with wet paper, dip other strips in the flour-and-water paste and cover the balloon with these. Put more layers of strips dipped in paste over the balloon. Hang it by the string to dry.

Cover the other balloon in the same way. Let the balloons dry for a day and a night.

After the paper is dry, stick a pin through it to pop the balloon. Now the large paper ball can be the owl's body, and the small one, the head.

Glue the head to the body.

Cut out cardboard wings, ears, and feet, and glue them in place. Paint on the eyes and the beak with poster paints.

hammers and saws

Pound with a hammer. Saw with a saw. Make boats, trains, puzzles, furniture, and many other useful things. They'll be all your own. Tools and wood are what you need. The next pages tell you how to make all sorts of things.

TOOLS FOR WORKING WITH WOOD

You need special tools to work with wood. Each tool has a special use, and each tool should be held correctly and used correctly.

Use a SAW to cut a straight line in wood.

Start the saw by drawing it back toward you at a slant. Hold the saw firmly, using a little pressure on the down stroke but none on the up stroke.

Use a COPING SAW to cut curved lines in wood.

The teeth should point toward the handle. The saw should be held straight up and down, not at a slant.

Use a HAMMER to pound nails into wood.

Grip the hammer firmly near the end of the handle when hitting a nail. Hit the nail squarely on the head so you won't bend it. If you bend a nail, use the claw end of the hammer to pry it up and start with another nail.

Use SANDPAPER to make wood smooth.

Use a C-CLAMP to hold your work in place. A vise on a workbench holds it even better.

GLUE also comes in handy when you are working with wood. There is a special glue for wood. It usually comes in a tube.

Use ENAMEL or TEMPERA paint to decorate the things you make from wood. Enamel takes a longer time to dry than tempera, but enamel won't rub or wash off. Tempera dries more quickly, but it will rub or wash off if you don't cover it with shellac.

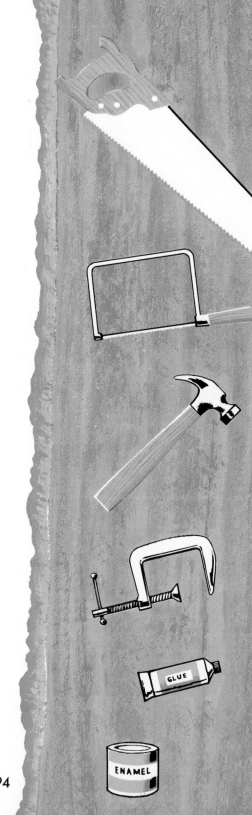

94

TAKE CARE OF YOUR TOOLS

Always keep your tools clean. Ask your father to help you oil them from time to time. Oil keeps them from getting rusty.

Put your tools away when you are not using them. A rack, like the one in the picture, is the best kind of place to keep them. You and your father can make one out of a big piece of pegboard.

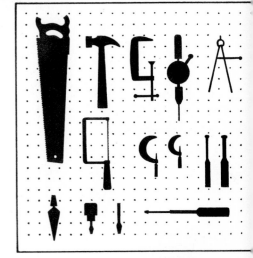

WHEELS

Some of the toys in this woodworking section need wheels.

You can buy small wooden wheels in a hobby store and in many dime stores. They are made in a number of sizes. Wheels about one-inch wide will be good for the toys in this book, though you can use larger or smaller wheels if you wish.

You may have to drill a hole in the center of each wheel for the nail that holds it to the toy. Use a hand drill to make the hole. The hole will be easier to drill if you use a vise or a C-clamp to hold the wheel to your worktable. The hole you drill should be a little larger than the nail that will act as an axle for the wheel on the toy.

If you can't buy wheels, you can make them out of empty spools by sawing the spools into several parts.

The hole in the center of the spool is larger than the heads of most nails. To keep the wheel from slipping off the nail, put a piece of cardboard or a washer on the outside of the wheel.

Materials
- a piece of wood for the main part of boat
- smaller pieces of wood for upper decks
- a round wooden rod for smokestacks

The materials you have will help you decide on the kind of boat you build. It may be long, short, narrow, wide, flat, or high.

FIRST MAKE THE PART OF YOUR BOAT THAT FLOATS

The bottom, or main part, of any boat is called its hull. All the other parts of a boat are built onto the hull. Make the hull from the largest piece of wood you have.

The bow, or front, of the hull is usually pointed. To make a point, saw the corners off one end of the wood. See Picture. Round the sides.

The stern, or rear, of the hull is often rounded. Use the coping saw, or even your file, to round off the corners of the stern. See Picture.

DECKS AND SMOKESTACKS

Nail small squares and oblong pieces of wood to the hull for as many more decks as you want. Use thin nails.

Nail short pieces of round rod to the top to make as many smokestacks as you want.

Smooth the boat with sandpaper before you paint it.

HOW TO MAKE AN AIRCRAFT CARRIER

The landing deck of an aircraft carrier is wider and longer than the hull. The deck of a real carrier holds about one hundred airplanes.

You can cut a landing deck from a thin piece of wood, like the wood in a cigar box. Nail the deck to the hull with thin nails.

SOME BOATS TO BUILD

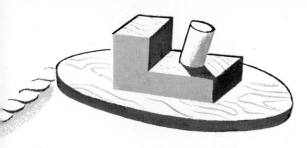

A tugboat is short and wide.

An ocean liner is long and narrow.

An ore boat is longer and narrower.

An aircraft carrier is the longest and narrowest.

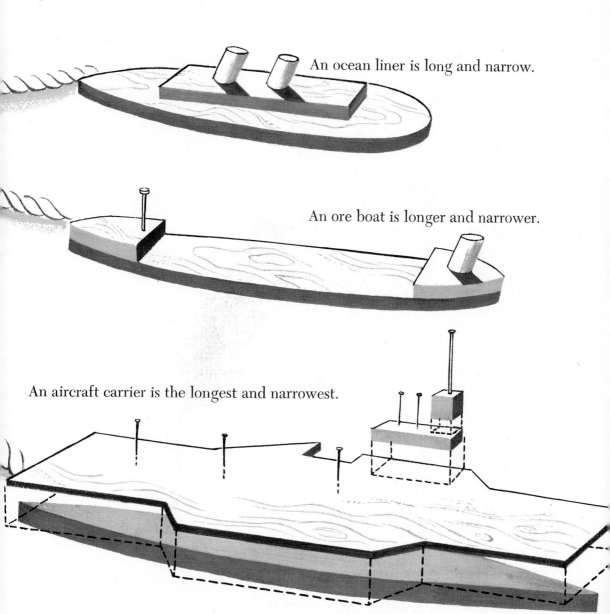

Notice that the pilot house, radio room, and other decks of an aircraft carrier are at the side of the landing deck. They are built there to leave room for the airplanes to take off.

Materials

- a scrap of lumber for the base, about 6 inches long and 4 inches wide
- large scraps of insulation board
- enamel paint
- a screw eye
- string
- paper

Pull-along pets make fine gifts for your little brother or sister.

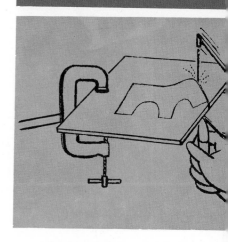

HOW TO MAKE THE BASE

The block of wood on which the toy pet stands is called the base. Rub it smooth with sandpaper. Then paint it whatever color you wish.

You will need four wheels for the base. On page 95 you will find out how to make the wheels. Paint them first. Then nail the wheels to the base. Do not pound the nails in too far or the wheels will not turn.

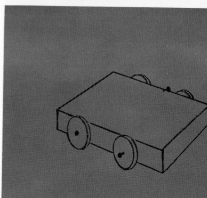

HOW TO MAKE THE TOY PET

Make a paper pattern by tracing the outline of any animal from a magazine or book. Or follow one of the pictures on this page.

Cut out your pattern.

Place the pattern on a piece of insulation board and draw around it.

Clamp the board with your vise or C-clamp to your worktable. Saw on the lines with a coping saw. To make the toy pet thicker, saw out other pieces from the same pattern and glue them together. Hold the pieces together with a clamp until they dry.

Sand the toy pet smooth and paint it.

Pound nails through the base and into the legs of the animal to hold it to the base. Or glue the animal to the base.

Add a screw eye to the front of the base for the pull string.

Dress the animal by gluing cloth or other materials to it. Felt, leather, or pieces of an old inner tube make spots for a giraffe, ears for an elephant, a mane for a lion, and arm-like wings for a penguin.

Pipe cleaners make good tails and tusks. Glue on sawdust, colored with vegetable dye, to make fur.

99

Materials

- a long piece of wood (2 by 4 inches is best)
- wheels (see page 95)
- screw hooks and screw eyes, one set for each car
- ½-inch-thick piece from round wooden rod, or spool, for smokestack

ENGINE

CABOOSE

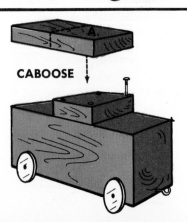

A
WOODEN
FREIGHT
TRAIN

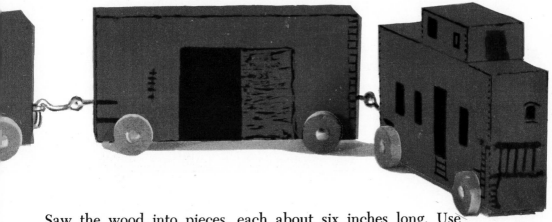

Saw the wood into pieces, each about six inches long. Use these pieces to make the whole train.

THE LOCOMOTIVE ENGINE

The engine has a cab for the engineer to sit in. It is higher than the front of the engine so that the engineer can see far ahead on the tracks. See the picture that shows how to draw the pattern for the engine. Saw out Section A.

THE CABOOSE

On top of a caboose is a little room which railroad men call the "crow's nest." You can use half of the piece you sawed out from the engine for the crow's nest. Glue it or nail it to the top of your caboose. See Picture.

THE WHOLE TRAIN

Sandpaper the engine, the caboose, and each of the other cars until the wood is smooth. Then paint them and paint the wheels. See the pictures for ideas on painting the cars.

Nail four wheels to each car, the engine, and the caboose.

Add screw hooks to the front and screw eyes to the back of each car for couplers. Glue pieces of round rod to the engine for the smokestack and the headlight as in the picture. Or use a spool for the smokestack.

RING-THE-BELL GAME

Materials

- an 8-inch piece of wood, 2 by 4 inches • a 16-inch piece of wood, 1 by 4 inches • a 4-inch piece of wood, 1 by 1 inches • a wooden slat 8 inches long • a piece of wire from a clothes hanger • a bell, the kind you buy in a pet shop • a large wooden bead • 2 strong rubber bands • 5 finishing nails • a black crayon • a hammer • a drill • a ruler • a pencil • friction tape

One of the amusements you will find at every carnival is a tall machine where you can test your strength by trying to hit a bell. You can make a small "Ring-the-Bell" game and have lots of fun with it.

HOW TO MAKE THE GAME

1. Draw twelve lines with crayon about an inch apart on the 16-inch piece of wood. Use crayon to number spaces. See Picture.

2. Make an "L" with 16-inch piece of wood which will be the back and 8-inch piece of wood which will be the base. Hammer 2 nails through the back of the "L" into the base. Now you have the stand.

3. Place wooden bead in center of base almost against back. Insert nail through hole in bead to make a mark. Drill a small hole in nail mark about an inch deep. Now make another nail mark the same way in top center of back. This time drill a hole straight through the back.

4. Slip clothes hanger wire through wooden bead and insert wire into hole at base. Bend top of wire and poke bent end through the back. Bend part of wire that sticks through the hole and cover with tape.

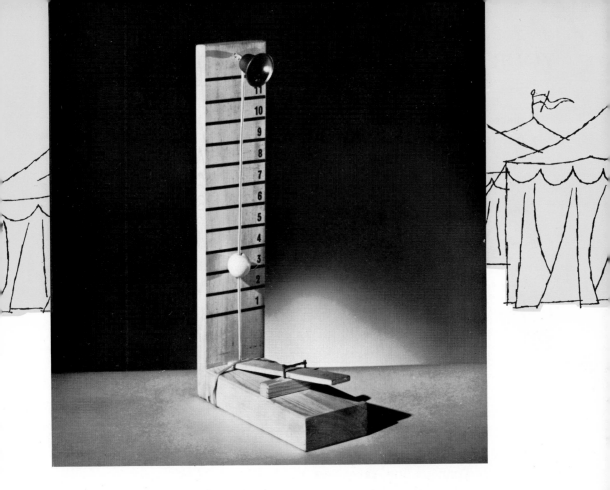

5. Place 4-inch piece of wood lengthwise across the base about 2 inches in from the open end.

6. Make a notch in the center at one end of 8-inch slat. Place slat on 4-inch piece of wood so that the notched end fits around wire. Hammer a nail on each side of where slat rests on raised 4-inch piece. Do not drive nails all the way in.

7. Hook one rubber band across the raised nail heads. Slip other strong rubber band around the base and over slat near the notched end.

8. Tie bell at top of wire. See Picture.

Hit the end of the slat to drive the bead up the wire. If it goes far enough, the bead will hit the bell. You and your friends can have lots of fun seeing how high you can drive the bead and how many times you can ring the bell.

YOUR OWN JIGSAW PUZZLE

Materials
- a piece of thin plywood
- a picture cut from a magazine
- all-purpose glue
- shellac

Glue the picture onto the plywood. Be sure to cover the back of the picture with glue. After you have glued the picture on the plywood, roll it with a rolling pin to take away the air bubbles.

After the glue is dry, brush the picture with clear shellac and let it dry.

Cut the puzzle pieces with a coping saw. Use a C-clamp or vise to hold the plywood to your worktable as you saw. When you use a coping saw, saw away from your body so you won't get cut.

Cut out as many puzzle pieces as you want. With your coping saw, you can make many interesting shapes out of the puzzle pieces.

Keep the puzzle in a cigar box when you are finished.

PING-PONG PADDLE

Materials
- thin plywood
- cardboard for pattern

Cut a paddle shape out of cardboard. See Picture. It can be any size, but it is best to have one that fits your hand easily. Try cutting several different-sized paddles from the cardboard to find out which fits best.

Trace around the cardboard pattern on the plywood.

Use a vise or C-clamp to hold the plywood to your worktable while you saw it with a coping saw.

Sand the edge of the paddle smooth.

With two paddles and a ball you can play a kind of tennis game with your friends.

PADDLE BALL

You can make a paddle and ball to play with by yourself.

You will need a paddle, some rubber bands, and a small rubber ball.

Loop the rubber bands together as shown. There should be enough of them looped together to stretch the length of your arm.

Nail or staple one end of the rubber band chain to the middle of the paddle. Ask your mother to sew the other end to the rubber ball. Or sew it yourself, if you can.

See how many times you can hit the ball in the air without missing.

FURNITURE
FOR YOUR ROOM

A DESK

With two crates and a board you can make a desk you will be proud of.

Stand two sturdy crates on end. They should be the same size. Lay a smooth piece of plywood across the crates for a desk top. Nail it down.

Rub away the rough spots with sandpaper. Add a coat or two of enamel to match your room, or use varnish. Now show off your new desk to your family and friends.

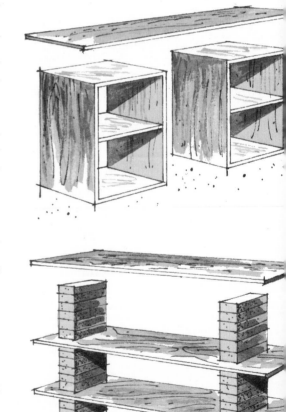

A BOOKSHELF

A bookshelf is easy to make with bricks and boards. Use stone bricks, glass bricks, or concrete blocks. Any kind of wooden boards will do.

Decide where you are going to put the shelf. Put some bricks on the floor and place a board on top of them. See Picture.

Stack the bricks as high as you want the next shelf to be. Lay a board on top of the bricks. Stack more bricks to make another shelf. Lay another board on top.

when you have a party

a party

Which game should you play at a party?
Magic Motions? Poor Pussy?
Unspin the Web?
What favors should you make?
How do you plan the best kind of party?
For a good time, see the ideas and the
games on these pages.

Give a party

You don't have to wait for your birthday or for a special occasion to have a party. You can have one any day of the year. Take your pick:

Birthday party
Kindergarten party
Mother Goose party
Cowboy party
Beach party
Picnic party

Circus party
Carnival party
Harvest party
Back-to-school party
Come-as-you-are party
Hobo party
Sandbox party
Space party
Wagon-train party
Buried-treasure party

110

Going-away party
Indian powwow party
Private-eye party
Boat party
Sailor party
Lollipop party
Soap-bubble party
Doll party
County-fair party

The games on the

following pages can be

played at any party.

before the party

1 Ask your parents for permission to have a party.

2 Decide what kind of party you want and whether it will be held indoors or outdoors.

3 Decide when to have the party.

4 Decide how long the party will last.

5 Decide whom you will invite to the party.

6 Send written invitations to your friends after your mother has found out if they can come. Tell them what kind of party you are having, at what time, where, and whether or not the guests should wear costumes.

You can use colored paper to make the invitations.

Ask your mother to help you put the names on the invitations.

7 Make decorations that fit the kind of party you are giving—flags for a Fourth-of-July party, a Santa Claus for a Christmas party, balloons for a circus party, or pumpkins cut from paper for a Halloween party.

8 Ask your mother to help you prepare the refreshments. Ice cream, cake, cookies, and lemonade are good for any party.

9 Make a list of games you would like to play. Choose some quiet games as well as running games.

10 Make party hats and favors for the guests. Or have the materials at the party and let the guests make their own.

PARTY HATS

from these . . .

paper plates

construction paper

paper bag

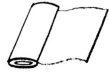

crepe paper

you can make . . .

sun hat

Indian hat

space helmet

party hat

sunflower hat

bunny hat

chef's hat

girl's
party hat

reindeer hat

beanie

Easter bonnet

sailor hat

baseball cap

crown

PARTY FAVORS

LOLLIPOP MAN

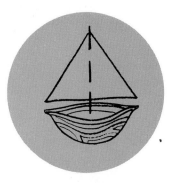

SAILBOAT

WATCH

SAND PAIL

TEPEE

WHISTLE

BUBBLE PIPE

FLOAT TOY

ROCKING HORSE

115

PARTY ANIMAL

ZOO

Before your guests come, hide peanuts around the room or the yard.

Separate the guests into three or four groups, and name each group for an animal, such as lion, bear, wolf, or donkey. Ask one guest in each group to be zookeeper.

When the player finds a peanut, he must not pick it up, but must make the same sound that the animal makes. Then the zookeeper gives him the peanut. The group that gets the most peanuts is the winner.

DUCKS FLY!

Choose one guest to be the leader and another to be the watcher. Have the others stand in a line facing them. The leader flaps his arms, honks like a duck, and calls out, "Ducks fly!" Then the guests flap their arms, honk like ducks, and say, "Ducks fly!" Or the leader might hop up and down and call out, "Rabbits hop!" Then the guests hop up and down and call out, "Rabbits hop!"

But if the leader should say, "Ducks meow!" or "Rabbits bark!" the guests must not follow him. Anyone who flaps his arms or hops up and down when he shouldn't becomes a watcher. When there is only one person left, he becomes the leader.

GAMES

POOR PUSSY

This game makes everybody laugh.

Have the guests sit around the room. Choose one person to be pussy. Pussy must go over to a guest and meow three times. The guest must pet pussy's head three times and say, "Poor pussy, poor pussy, poor pussy," without laughing.

The pussy should do his best to make the guest laugh. He can make funny meows and walk around like a cat. The pussy goes from one guest to another until someone laughs.

The first one to laugh becomes the new pussy.

TAP THE BEAR

Choose one guest to be the bear and another to be his guard.

The bear sits in a chair in the middle of a circle of guests. The guard stands behind his chair.

The guests try to tap the bear and to return to their places before the guard touches them. The first guest that the guard touches becomes the next bear If the guard does not touch the guest before he taps the bear, the bear is free—and the guard must be the bear.

Choose another guard and continue the game until everyone has been the bear.

117

LISTEN and MOVE GAMES

MUSIC-STOP-SQUAT

In this game each player must stop moving—and squat—fast.

Have someone play the piano or put on a record.

Choose one guest to be the spotter.

Then have everyone march around the room in time to the music. Stop the music! Everyone must squat. The last one to squat is out of the game. He must become the spotter and catch the last squatter in the next game.

RIVER RAT

Lay a small rug in the middle of the room for a river. Or draw two chalk lines on the floor to mark the sides of the river.

Choose one person to be the watcher.

Have everyone line up on one side of the river. Start the music and have everyone march across the river.

Stop the music!

Anyone standing in the river is the river rat. He steps out of the line and watches for other river rats who get caught in the river.

JACK-IN-THE-BOX

Choose one person for the leader.

Have the others stand in a wide circle around him.

When the leader calls, "Jack-in-the-box," all squat.

When the leader calls, "Jack-out-of-the-box," all jump up.

The leader can trick the others by calling out the directions slowly or quickly, or by repeating the same one when no one expects it.

Players who do not follow the leader are out of the game. The best listener is the last one left in the game, and he becomes the leader for the next game.

MAGIC MOTIONS

Have everyone sit in a circle.

Choose one person to be the guesser, and ask him to leave the room. Then choose another person to be the leader.

The leader starts the game by clapping. Everyone claps. When the guesser hears this, he can come back into the room. He must stand in the center of the circle and try to guess which person is the leader.

The leader can change motions. He can make all kinds of funny motions, such as waving one finger, or making funny faces. Everyone follows the leader.

The guesser gets three guesses to find the leader. If he guesses right, he can choose the next leader.

119

HOT POTATO

Choose someone to be IT. Set enough chairs in a circle for all your guests except IT. He must stand in the center of the circle.

The guests throw a wadded piece of newspaper or a beanbag back and forth across the circle. This is the "hot potato." If IT can catch the hot potato while it is in the air, he gets the thrower's seat, and the thrower is IT.

HOT SEAT

Set enough chairs in a circle for all your guests. Choose one player to be IT. Have him stand in the center of the circle. His empty seat is the "hot seat." The players should change seats again and again to prevent IT from sitting down.

At any time IT can call out, "All move," and all the players will have to move over one seat. This gives IT a better chance to get a seat.

When IT gets a seat, the player whose seat he takes is the new IT.

CATCH THE CANE

Place chairs in a circle for all your guests except one. The one who doesn't get a seat is IT. He stands in the center of the circle with a cane or a stick that has one end resting on the floor.

IT calls out the name of someone sitting in a chair and then lets go of the cane. This person must catch the cane before it hits the floor. If he doesn't catch it, he is IT. If he catches the cane, IT calls another name.

HOT AND COLD

Have the guests sit in a circle. Give each one a knife, a fork, or a spoon, and a tin can or a pan.

Choose one player to be the guesser and have him leave the room. While he is out, the other players choose an object he is to look for in the room, such as a book, a doorknob, or a window. When the players start to beat softly on the cans, the guesser can return. He should look and look all over the room. When he gets close to what the players have chosen, they beat louder and louder on the cans. When he walks away from it, they beat softer and softer.

After the guesser finds the chosen object, he names someone else to go out of the room.

PAPER-CUT RACE

BALLOON RACES

CLOTHES RACE

FEATHER FLY

races

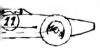

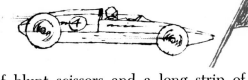

PAPER-CUT RACE

You need a pair of blunt scissors and a long strip of crepe paper for each player. All the strips should be the same length.

Tie one end of each strip to something like a chair or a stair post. Or pin the ends to a cushion.

Give each player the other end and the scissors.

When you say, "Go!" the players can start cutting along the middle of the paper. The first one to reach the other end of his strip is the winner.

BALLOON RACES

Give each player a blown-up balloon. Have everyone get down on hands and knees behind a starting line. When you give the signal, the players start toward the finish line, pushing the balloons in front of them with their noses. The first one to reach the finish line with his balloon is the winner.

For another balloon race, have your guests blow up balloons. The one who has blown up the largest balloon when you say, "Stop!" is the winner.

CLOTHES RACE

Have your guests pick partners. Place a closed suitcase (or large paper sack) several yards in front of each pair. Various articles of clothing are already in the suitcase, such as boots, gloves, coats, and bathrobes. Be sure the clothes are large enough to put on over the players' regular clothing.

Each pair leaves the starting line at a given signal. They run to their suitcase, open it, and put on everything inside. Then they run back to the starting point, turn, and race back to the suitcase. They take off the clothes, put them back in the suitcase, and return to the starting point. The first pair to cross the finish line wins.

FEATHER FLY

Give each player a small feather (or crumpled piece of tissue paper) and a fan. Using his fan, a player must guide his feather from the starting line to the turning point and back to the finish. At no time is he allowed to touch his feather.

123

TAGS **and**

TAG

Choose someone to be IT.
He chases the guests until he catches
someone to be IT.
Here are more ways to play tag:
Walking tag—everyone must walk—fast!
Skip tag—everyone must skip.
Jump tag—everyone must jump.
Hop tag—everyone must hop.
Squat tag—no one can be tagged if he
squats before IT touches him.
Kneel tag—no one can be tagged if he
kneels and puts his forehead on the floor.
Stand-still tag—when IT catches someone,
the new IT stands on the spot
where he was tagged and tries to
touch the others as they run by him.
Ostrich tag—no one can be tagged if
he has his right arm under his right leg,
and is holding his nose with his right hand.
Nose-and-Toe tag—no one can be tagged if
he holds his nose with one hand and
his toes with the other.
Seat-change tag—everyone sits on the floor
in a circle. IT stands in the center.
IT calls the names of two persons
in the circle. They must change seats.
IT tries to get one of their seats.
If a person loses his seat, he is the new IT.

RACES

RELAY RACES

Mark off start and finish lines, a running distance apart.

Line up the guests into two groups, with the same number of people in each group. One person from each group races to the finish line and comes back to tag the next person in line. The first group to have everyone finish is the winner.

POTATO ROLL

Line up the guests behind a starting line. Have them push potatoes along the ground with a stick or spoon. Or they can push peanuts with their noses. The first one to reach the finish line is the winner.

ANIMAL RACES

In this race everyone walks like an animal. They can hop like rabbits, gallop like horses, or waddle like ducks, but everyone must do the same animal walk in each race. The first one to finish, using the animal walk, is the winner.

What You Need

- pennies, checkers, or small flat pebbles
- can lids or plates
- a large dishpan or plastic swimming pool

Fill a large dishpan with water. Float can lids on the water.

Set the pan on the ground, and have the players line up a few feet away.

Give each player 10 pennies, 10 checkers, or 10 small pebbles to throw into the lids. The player who gets the most pennies in the lids is the winner.

Roll, pitch, and toss games

ROLL-THE-BALL GAME

What You Need

- a pencil
- 3 small rubber balls or golf balls
- a large cardboard carton
- poster paints • tape

Cut the flaps from a cardboard carton. Draw two bunnies with big feet on the side of the carton. See Picture. The heads can be made from the flaps and taped in place. Cut holes in the feet large enough for a ball to roll through.

Paint the bunnies and the box. Put black score numbers over the holes.

Have each player stand a few feet away from the box and roll three balls, one at a time. Each time a player rolls a ball through one of the holes, he makes that score. The player with the highest number of points wins.

PITCH-THE-BALL GAME

What You Need

- a pencil
- 3 small rubber balls
- a large cardboard carton
- poster paints • tape

Cut the flaps from a cardboard carton. Turn the carton upside down. Draw two clown heads with wide-open mouths on the carton. Then draw a balloon floating over the heads.

Cut holes in the mouths and in the balloon. Make the holes of three different sizes, all bigger than your ball.

Paint the carton, the clowns and the balloon. Put numbers near the mouth and balloon holes. The higher numbers should be near the smaller holes.

Set the box on a table or a barrel, against a wall or tree.

Have each player stand a few feet away and pitch three balls at the holes. The player who gets the highest score wins.

HUNT, FOLLOW

UNSPIN THE WEB

You will need a long string for each guest to unwind. Fasten one end of the string to a piece of furniture and hide a prize there. Wind the rest of the string over and under furniture around the room. Do this with each string.

Give the loose end to the guest and let him unwind the string until he comes to the prize.

FIND THE PUZZLE

This is a good game for a small party. Cut pictures from magazines into puzzle pieces. Make enough for every guest to have a puzzle picture. Hide all the pieces —except one—for each puzzle. Give this piece to the guest and let him find the others. When he finds all the pieces, he can put the puzzle together and get a prize.

AND FIND

FOLLOW THE ARROWS

An arrow trail is fun to follow. Lay it out with chalk, sticks, or leaves. You can make the trail easy or hard to follow. You can even trick the players by putting two arrows at the same place, one turning the wrong way.

At the end of the arrow trail, hide a party favor, a small toy, or a popcorn ball wrapped in cellophane.

BIG-GAME HUNT

Hide animal crackers or cardboard animals around the room. Then tell each player what animal he must find.

A box of animal crackers or cardboard animals is a good prize for those who find their animals.

Games for outdoors

DODGE BALL

Have everyone stand in a circle. Choose two, three, or four people to be dodgers. They will stand in the center of the circle and dodge the ball.

The others, who are rollers, toss a large ball to one another around the circle. Suddenly, a roller rolls the ball toward the dodgers. If the roller hits a dodger, the roller becomes a dodger.

TWIRL 'EM STATUES

You will need lots of room to play this game.

Choose one person to be the twirler and another person to be the buyer. Everyone else will be statues.

The twirler swings each person around by the arm and then lets go of him. Each person must hold the position he is in when he stops twirling. He must stand as still as a statue.

The buyer picks out the best statue, the funniest statue, or the prettiest statue. Statues that move will not be bought.

JUMP HIGH!

The person who can jump the highest wins this game.

Have two persons hold the ends of a rope. Line up the others to jump over the rope. Start with the rope on the ground. Raise it a little higher after everyone jumps over it. Then raise it higher, again and again. Be sure to hold the rope loosely so no one will trip over it.

The higher the rope is held, the fewer people can jump over it. The one who jumps the highest is the winner.

presents and surprises

Scraps of paper, balloons, cardboard box tops, and sipping straws—use these and other things to make gifts and decorations that will surprise your friends.

Table Mats

ROPE MATS

Materials
- clothesline • shellac
- thick-boiled starch • scissors
- tempera paints • wax paper • a pin

Ask your mother to help you make some thick-boiled starch. While the starch is cooling, spread out a piece of wax paper to work on.

Cut a piece of clothesline about six feet long.

When the starch is no longer hot, but is still warm, dip the rope in it.

Wind the starched rope into a flat coil on top of the wax paper. Flatten the coil as you wind it.

When the rope is all coiled, put a pin in the end to keep it from unwinding.

When the rope is dry, lift it off the wax paper. Now you have your mat. If you wish, you can take out the pin and put a dab of paste in its place.

Decorate the mat with tempera paints. Cover both sides with shellac.

The shellac will keep dishes that are hot or wet from smearing your design.

BURLAP TABLE MATS

Materials
- 1 or 2 burlap bags • starch
- scissors • tempera paint • shellac

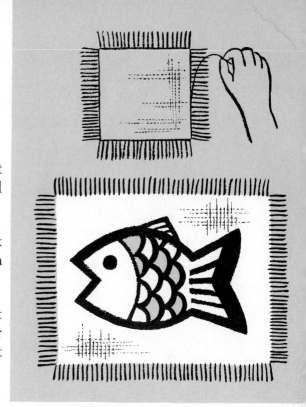

Cut out pieces the size of a table mat from the burlap bags. Soak in starch and let dry.

Paint designs on the mats. Do not mix water with the tempera paint when painting on burlap.

After the paint dries, cover each mat with shellac. If you wish, pull two or three threads from each side of the mat for a fringe.

WAX-PAPER MATS

Materials
- a roll of wax paper • scissors
- colored paper • an electric iron

Tear two sheets of wax paper from a roll. Each should be about as long as your arm.

Cut circles, squares, and other designs from colored paper. Place the designs between two sheets of wax paper.

Ask your mother to help you press the wax paper with a warm iron. The heat will seal the two wax sheets with the designs inside. Trim around the edges with scissors to complete your mat.

You can also draw designs on a sheet of white paper and seal it between the two sheets of wax paper to make a mat. Be sure that the white paper is smaller than the wax-paper sheets.

133

WASTEPAPER BASKET

Materials
- shellac • scissors • pictures
- an empty potato-chip or popcorn can
- shelf paper or candy wrappers • glue

Take the lid off an empty can. Cut a piece of shelf paper long enough to go around the can and lap over itself. The paper should be as wide as the can is high. Draw pictures on it, or leave it plain. Glue the shelf paper in place around the can.

Another way to decorate the can is to glue magazine pictures to it. Paste these all over the outside of the can. Each one should lap over another to make an interesting and attractive design. Finish the wastepaper basket with shellac.

Useful Gifts

DISPLAY OR SERVING TRAY

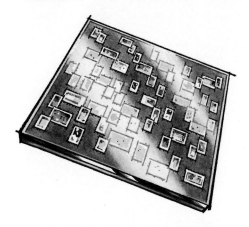

Materials
- a piece of clear glass or plastic about 10 inches square • a piece of soft felt the same size • used postage stamps • glue • brush • pencil

Wipe the glass or plastic clean of fingerprints. Brush glue onto the face of a stamp and place it against the glass or plastic. Roll it with a pencil to remove any air bubbles. Glue all your stamps on in this way, overlapping some of them. After the stamps have dried, glue the felt over them.

PEN-AND-PENCIL HOLDER

Materials
- corrugated paper • tape • scissors • a jar lid • shellac • poster paints

Cut a strip of corrugated paper about five inches wide. Make a tube with it around the lid of a jar. Tape the tube together.

Push the lid to the bottom of the tube and tape it in place.

Decorate the pencil holder, and shellac it to protect the design.

Put one or two pencils in the holder, and you have a useful gift.

A STRING HOLDER

Materials
- a paper plate • crayons or paint • string • scissors • tape

Cut a paper plate in half. One-half of a plate will make one string holder. Decorate it. Then twist the half into a cone shape, and tape it together.

Cut off the point of the cone to make a hole for the string to come through. Shellac the cone to protect the decoration.

Put a ball of string in the top of the cone. The end of the string can stick through the hole in the bottom.

Now you have a string holder to hang on the wall.

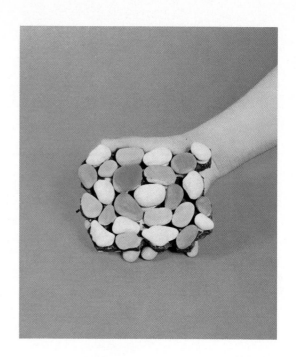

A Paperweight

Materials
• 15 or 20 small stones, each about the size of a peanut shell or a jellybean • a piece of cork or heavy cardboard about as big as your hand • white liquid glue • poster paints and brush • shellac

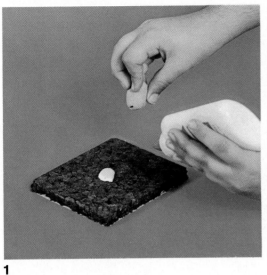

1

2

1. Glue one of the larger stones to the center of the cork or the cardboard.
2. Glue other stones in a circle around the center stone. You can make more than one circle. You can also glue one stone on top of another to make more than one layer.
3. Let the glue dry. Paint each stone. When the paint dries, shellac each stone. Let the shellac dry to a hard, shiny finish.
4. Cut away most of the cork or cardboard that sticks out beyond the edges of the stones. You now have a paperweight for yourself or a friend.

3

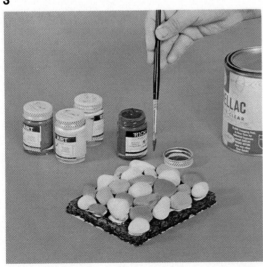

4

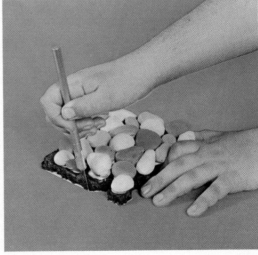

baskets

A FOLDED PAPER BASKET

Fold a sheet of paper in half the long way. Fold it in half again. Now unfold the sheet and fold it in half the short way. Then fold it in half again. Unfold, and there will be six creases as in Picture 1.

Now refold along the creases (Picture 2).

Fold corner flaps (Picture 3).

Fold the tabs on the ends (Picture 4).

The basket is pulled into shape (Picture 5).

Make a paper handle for the basket. Paste it on securely. If you turn the basket over, you have a party hat.

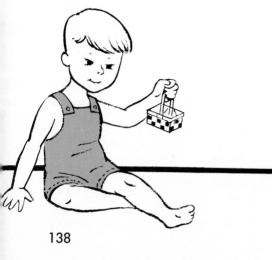

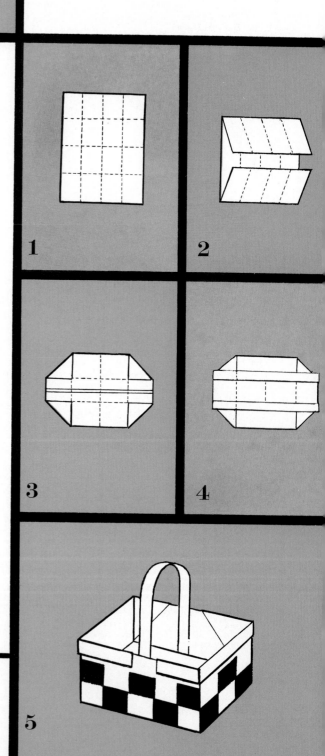

1

2

3

4

5

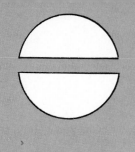

A CONE-SHAPED BASKET

Materials
- heavy paper   • ribbon or string   • a plate   • a pencil   • paste

Use a half circle of paper to make the cone basket. To make a half circle, draw a whole circle on paper, using a plate as the pattern. Cut out the circle and fold it in half. Cut the two halves apart along the fold (Picture 1).

Twist the half circle into a cone shape and paste it in place (Picture 2).

Use a ribbon or a string for the handle. Paste the ends of the ribbon in place (Picture 3).

Decorate your cone basket.

OTHER EASY BASKETS

The bottom of a milk carton makes a good-looking basket. A paper plate also makes a good basket.

And you can decorate little plastic or wooden berry baskets with crepe-paper strips. Use pipe cleaners for handles.

139

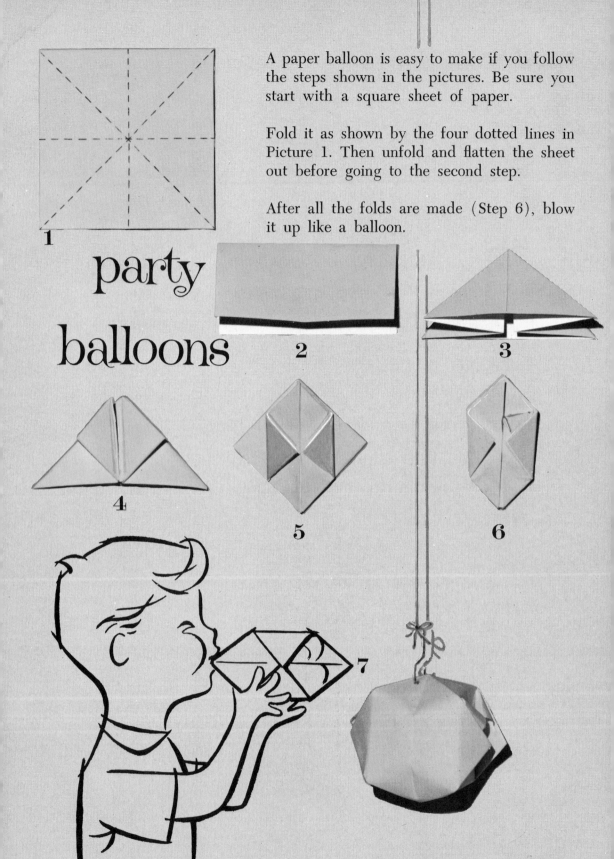

A paper balloon is easy to make if you follow the steps shown in the pictures. Be sure you start with a square sheet of paper.

Fold it as shown by the four dotted lines in Picture 1. Then unfold and flatten the sheet out before going to the second step.

After all the folds are made (Step 6), blow it up like a balloon.

party balloons

1

2

3

4

5

6

7

PARTY HATS

Again start with a square sheet of paper. Fold it in half for the first step.

To make larger hats, use larger squares of paper.

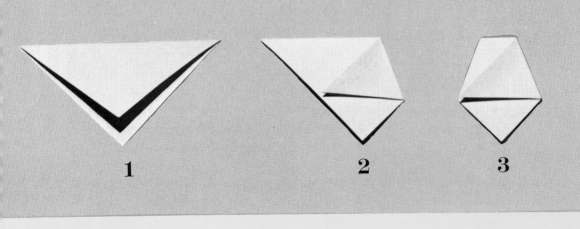

1

2

3

4

5

6

7

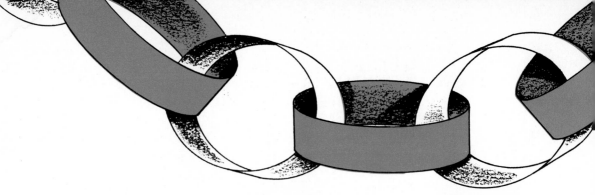

paper-ring chain

Materials
- colored paper • scissors • paste

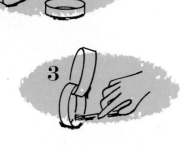

1. Cut your paper into strips, each four or five inches long.

2. Take one strip of paper and make a ring with it. Paste the ends together.

3. Make another ring with the next strip of paper, linking it with the first ring.

Add more and more rings to make the chains as long as you want.

The paper rings can also be made of white paper decorated with crayons, of shiny tin foil, or of paper in different colors.

Trim each ring with bits of sparkly paper and glitter if you wish. Then the chain will sparkle in the light.

a folding fan

Materials
- a piece of paper
- crayons • a paper clip

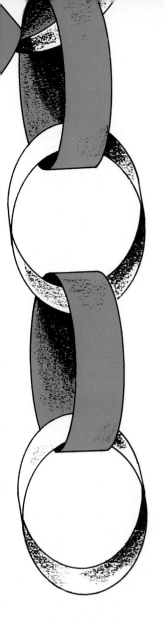

sipping-straw chains

Materials
- colored paper
- a blunt needle
- sipping straws
- scissors
- yarn

1. Ask your mother to thread a long piece of yarn on a blunt needle. Perhaps you can do it yourself. Knot the end of the yarn.

2. Cut several sipping straws into short pieces. Cut the colored paper into pieces of different shapes.

3. String a paper, then a straw, then a paper, then a straw. Make the chain any length you wish.

Fold the paper back and forth so that it looks like an accordion.

Unfold and decorate any way you want.

Fold again and put a paper clip on one end. Use it as a tree decoration or for dress-up.

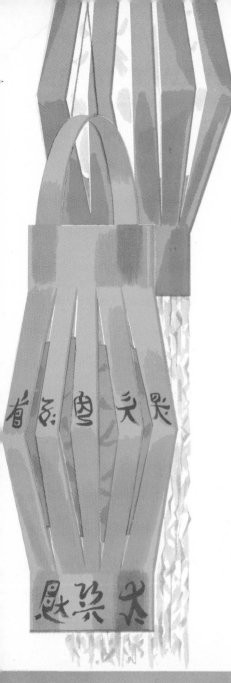

japanese lanterns

Materials
- a piece of heavy paper (colored construction paper is good)
- scissors • paste or a stapler

Cut a narrow strip from the end of your paper for the lantern handle. Put it aside.

Fold the paper in half the long way. Cut slits across the fold.

Unfold the paper and bend into a circle. Paste or staple the ends together where they meet.

Paste or staple the handle strip to the top of the lantern. You can trim the lantern with bits of foil or tinsel.

Put a piece of crumpled red tissue or crepe paper inside the lantern to make it look lighted.

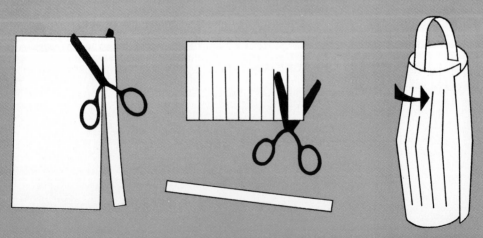

paper-loop balls

Materials
- paper
- scissors
- string
- paste or a stapler

Cut three narrow strips of paper, each about the length of a new pencil.

Bend each strip into a ring, and paste or staple the ends together.

Put the three rings together to form a ball.

Paste or staple them together where the three rings meet at the top and bottom.

Tie, paste, or staple a little loop of string to the top of the paper ball. You can hang the ball by this loop.

If you wish, you can decorate the ball with bits of foil and tinsel.

glitter balls

Materials
- cellophane straws
- thread or string
- scissors

Cut six or eight cellophane straws in half. Put all the halves together in a pile. The ends should be even.

Tie a thread or string around the middle of the pile. Pull the string tight.

As the string is pulled tight, it will squeeze the straws, and the ends of the straws will spread out in all directions.

You can hang the glitter ball by the string.

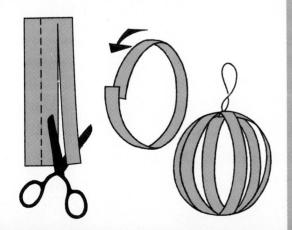

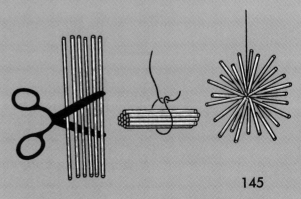

145

Christmas Tree Decorations

Angel

Materials

- shiny shelf paper, any color
- scissors • a pencil • cotton
- some things to make large and small circle patterns, such as plates and coins
- white paper • a stapler
- paste

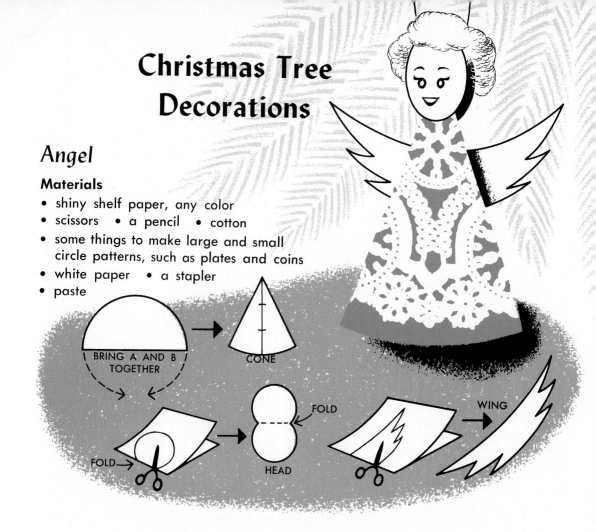

Draw a large circle on shelf paper using a large circle pattern. Cut out the circle, and fold it in half.

Cut the circle in half along the fold.

Bend the half circle into a cone, bringing Corners A and B together as in the picture. Fasten it in place with staples or paste.

Fold a sheet of white paper. Put the small circle pattern on the paper, with the edge of the circle at the fold. Draw around the circle and cut it out, but do not cut across the fold. When you unfold the paper, you will have two circles fastened to each other. See Picture.

Draw a face on one of the small circles. Paste cotton hair to the other.

Paste the bottom of each circle to the top of the cone.

Fold another piece of shelf paper. Draw a wing at the fold as shown. Cut it out. Unfold and paste or staple the double wing across the angel's back.

You can hang your angel up with a string loop attached to the head.

Fuzzy Snowman

Materials
- stiff white paper or thin cardboard
- Christmas tree snow, the kind you buy in a dime store
- a pencil or a black crayon
- glue • string

Glue

Hat

String

PASTE TOP OF
HEAD BETWEEN
BOTTOM OF HAT

Draw three circles on stiff paper. Make one big circle, one middle-sized circle, and one small circle. Cut out all three circles.

Paste the three circles together as shown in the picture.

Draw in a face. Draw buttons on the snowman. Cut a hat out of paper and put it on the snowman's head. The hat can be colored black.

Cover the snowman with glue. Try not to put glue where the buttons and the facemarks are.

Now, sprinkle the snowman with the store snow. The snow will stick to the wet glue. Let it dry, and tie a string to the top of the snowman so that you can hang it from a tree.

PIPE-CLEANER
Candy Canes

Materials
- red crepe paper or a red ribbon
- a pipe cleaner
- scissors
- paste

GLUE END FIRST
THEN WRAP
AROUND

Bend a pipe cleaner into a cane shape.

Cut a thin strip of crepe paper.

Wind the strip on a slant around the pipe cleaner. Glue the ends to the pipe cleaner.

Hang the cane on a Christmas tree.

Greeting Cards

hidden treasure

Materials
- a pencil • scissors • a penny • paste
- 4 pieces of paper, a little larger than this page

Cut a square out of each piece of paper. Each square should be a different size.

Fold each square into a little packet, as shown.

Open all the squares. Put one on top of another, the largest on the bottom and the smallest on top.

Paste the center of each square to the one below it.

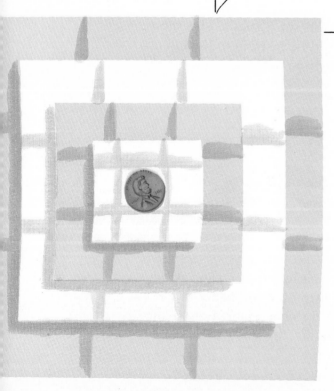

Paste the penny in the center of the smallest one. Each packet will be hidden by the next larger one.

Write messages on top of each fold, all the way down to the penny.

One can read, "Turn this flap up," another, "Open the door."

The more paper squares you have, the more fun your card will be to unwrap.

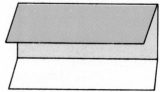 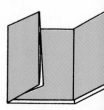

spiral card

Materials
- string • scissors • paste
- a piece of heavy colored paper • a pencil
- a small piece of white paper for the message

A message is hidden in this easy-to-make spiral greeting card.

Fold the colored paper in half.

Poke a hole with your scissors in the middle of the front half of the paper. Now cut a spiral with the scissors, around and around and out from the center hole. Turn the paper as you cut. See Picture. You might find it easier to do if you practice on a scrap of paper first.

Paste white paper on the inside back half of the folded paper, under the spiral. Write a message on it. Lift the spiral to make sure that the message can be seen, and then let it snap back in place, covering the message.

Use a dab of paste to fasten a string to the center of the spiral. Also, paste the corners of the folded paper together so that your card can be opened by lifting the spiral.

feel-it card

You can make greeting cards by gluing bits of cotton, felt, or other materials to a folded sheet of paper. A Santa Claus can have a cotton beard. An Easter rabbit can have a cotton tail.

You can also dye sawdust with vegetable dye. Then sprinkle it on a glue-covered spot on the card. Glitter from the dime store can also be glued to a card in this way.

149

AN ACCORDION CARD

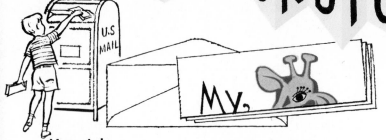

Materials
- scissors • a pencil • crayons • tape
- a piece of heavy paper, a little larger than this page

Cut your paper in half the long way. Tape the end of one half to the end of the other to make a long strip.

Draw a long-necked giraffe, snake, or other long animal stretching from one end of the card to the other. Color it.

Fold the card accordion style.

Now write a birthday message on the folds so that the person who gets your card can read it as he opens each fold.

My,

How

You

have

Grown

Happy

Birthday

Suzi

puzzle card

Materials
- scissors • cardboard
- an envelope • paste • crayons
- a sheet of white paper or a magazine picture

Draw a picture on a sheet of paper, or cut out a picture from some magazine. Paste this picture on a piece of cardboard. Write the greeting on the picture with a dark crayon.

Use scissors to cut the picture into puzzle pieces.

Put the pieces in an envelope and send it to your friend.

He will have fun putting the puzzle together to read your greeting.

Get Well Soon!

I MISS YOU

150

stunts and magic tricks

Can you make a thread rise in the air?
Can you make a seed bob up and down in a glass?
Can you make a handkerchief or a knot appear from nowhere?
The next pages show you how to do these tricks and many more, and there are stunts you can do, too.

funny

Here's how to walk like an animal.

ELEPHANT WALK

Stand with your feet apart. Bend over and put your hands flat on the floor without bending your knees. Keep your arms and legs straight. Walk with heavy steps.

DUCK WALK

Squat like the girl in the picture. Stretch your arms out to the sides. Now put your hands under your chin—and you have wings like a duck. Walk with heavy steps and wave your arms as if they were wings.

KANGAROO HOP

Squat and fold your arms in front of your chest. Jump as high and as far as you can. Be sure to bend your knees when you land.

animal walks

CRAB WALK

Squat, reach back, and put your hands on the floor behind you—without sitting down. Keep your back straight. Walk backwards, moving your right hand and right foot at the same time, and your left hand and left foot together. Practice until you can walk faster and faster. Then try running backwards.

SEAL WALK

Lie down on your stomach. Place your hands flat on the floor with your fingers turned to the side. Push on your hands until you have raised your body and until your arms are straight. Then walk around on your hands, dragging your feet behind you.

RABBIT HOP

Squat and put your arms between your legs with your hands on the floor. Push with your feet and jump, taking your hands off the floor. Land on your hands first and then your feet. Bring your feet toward your hands for another jump. Soon you can hop fast—just like a rabbit.

153

SIT, SQUAT, AND STAND ROLLS

INDIAN SIT

FROM A SQUAT TO A SQUAT

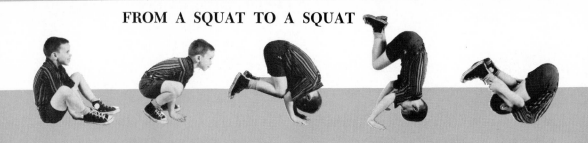

FROM A STAND TO A STAND

ROLL, ROLL, ROLL

INDIAN SIT

Squat with your knees apart at the edge of a mat or on a soft spot of grass. Put your hands flat in front of your feet. Put your chin on your chest and round your back. Push with both hands and both feet until you start to roll. As you roll over, cross your legs. End the roll sitting like an Indian.

For a good Indian sit, the top of your head should not touch the mat. Keep working at the stunt until you do a roll on your shoulders with most of your weight on your hands and arms.

FROM A SQUAT TO A SQUAT

Squat and put both hands flat in front of your feet. Round your back and put your chin on your chest. Push with your hands and feet until you start to roll. Keep your knees bent to land in a squat.

FROM A STAND TO A STAND

Stand tall. Spread your feet apart and squat. Round your back and put your chin on your chest. Push with your hands and feet until you start to roll. Keep your knees bent until you land in a squat. Then straighten your knees and stand tall.

ROLL, ROLL, ROLL

Once you have learned to do the forward rolls, you can do them one after another. You will need a large mat or a long strip of soft grass.

Try rolling with crossed legs to an Indian sit over and over again to the end of the mat. Or roll from a squat to a squat without standing up. You can do a number of rolls from a stand to a stand. Try putting all of these rolls together. Do an Indian sit, a squat to a squat, and a stand to a stand, one after another to the end of the mat.

After you have learned to do squats, sits, and stand rolls, try doing a roll from a slow walk. Be sure to use your hands to carry you over and tuck your chin on your chest. When you can do this stunt easily, go on to a faster walk. Soon you can do rolls from a run.

stunts for two

WHEELBARROW

Let the smaller person be the wheelbarrow and the other be the lifter. The wheelbarrow puts his hands on the floor and keeps his legs straight. The lifter stands at his feet. He picks up one leg of the wheelbarrow and then the other, tucking both feet under his arms. The wheelbarrow starts walking on his hands. When he wants to stop, he lowers one leg at a time.

If enough people are doing stunts, you can have wheelbarrow races.

LEAP FROG

Ask your friend to get down on his hands and knees and make himself as small as he can. You stand at his feet and place both hands on his back. Jump into the air, spread your legs apart, and leap over your friend. Then get down on your hands and knees, and have your friend jump over you.

BACK-TO-BACK

Sit on the floor back to back with some-one. Lock your arms together like the boy and girl in the picture. Push against each other and stand up. Push against each other again and sit down. See how many times you can do this stunt.

ROCKING HORSE

You and your partner sit on the floor facing each other. Sit far enough apart so that you can sit on each other's feet keeping your knees straight.

Grasp hands and rock back and forth, one of you pulling when the other is pushing. As you rock back, raise your feet and your partner will rise in the air. When he rocks back, you rise in the air. Keep rocking back and forth to see how high you can go.

TRICKS WITH PAPER

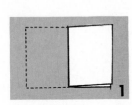

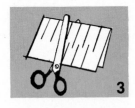

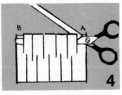

A Paper-Cutting Trick

THE TRICK

Announce that you are going to put your head through a hole you will cut in a small piece of paper you hold in your hand. The paper can be as small as two inches by five-and-one-half inches. It looks impossible!

HOW YOU DO IT

The secret is the way you cut the paper. Fold the paper the long way. With the folded side toward you, cut about 12 slits through the fold. See Picture 2. Be careful not to cut all the way across the paper.

Turn the paper around so the edges are facing you. Cut another row of slits between the first slits. See Picture 3.

Finally, cut along the fold, starting at A and stopping at B. See Picture 4. Begin cutting at the first slit and stop at the last slit. Do not cut through the edges of the paper. Unfold it and put it on.

Pencil Magic

Ask a friend to write the number 1000—without lifting his pencil from the paper. No matter how he tries, he cannot do it.

When he gives up, show him how it can be done by folding the edge of the paper down, and by drawing the figure shown.

A Paper-Tearing Trick

Hold up a piece of paper with two slits torn in it. Ask someone who thinks he is strong to finish tearing the paper. It looks easy, but it cannot be done.

Ask the person to hold the paper by the corners and tear BOTH ends from the middle piece with ONE pull. After a few tugs, the person will give up. He cannot tear off more than one end with one pull.

MIND READING
AND TRICKS
OF MYSTERY

THE TRICK

Ask someone to think of either his right or his left hand while you stand with your back to him. Tell him to hold this hand to his forehead and think hard.

After about a minute, ask him to lower his hand. Turn and face him. Immediately, tell him which hand he was thinking about.

HOW YOU KNOW

The hand he held to his forehead will be whiter. The blood has rushed out of it.

THE MYSTERIOUS THREAD

THE TRICK

Make a thread rise in the air.

HOW YOU DO IT

Hold a piece of thread in one hand and a plastic comb in the other. Run the comb through someone's hair. Then hold it above the piece of thread. The thread will rise in the air. If you move the comb, the thread will follow it. (To you it is no mystery—just static electricity.)

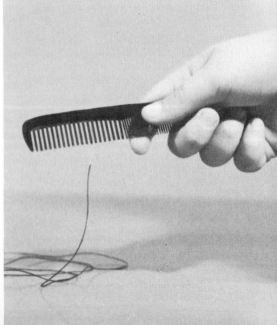

READING SEALED MESSAGES

THE TRICK

Ask everyone to write a wish on a piece of paper and fold it. You will hold the folded paper up and guess the wish.

HOW YOU DO IT

You can do this mind-reading trick for many persons, but one of them must be your secret helper. Your helper writes a wish that the two of you have agreed upon ahead of time, such as a wish for a horse. Everyone folds his paper and places it in a hat or box. Your helper puts a special mark on his paper.

When all the folded papers are collected, pick any one of them, except the one with your helper's mark on it.

1. Hold the paper over your head, pretend to think hard, and say, "Someone wished for a horse." Your helper will stand up and say that he wished for a horse.

2. Open the paper. Read the message to yourself. The message will not be your helper's, but someone else's. Look at the message and say, "Yes, you did wish for a horse." But you have really just read the next person's wish.

3. Now pick up another paper (not your helper's). Hold the paper over your head and pretend to think hard. Then you repeat the wish you read before, which might be a wish for candy. The person who wrote this wish will stand up and say you are right. Read the next wish when you open the paper. Save your helper's wish for last.

161

Tricks with Rope and String

A ROPE TRICK

THE TRICK

Ask someone to tie a knot in a rope without letting go of either end. The person will think it is impossible, but you know how to do it.

HOW YOU DO IT

Give the person a piece of rope about three feet long and tell him to hold one end in each hand. Ask him to tie a knot in the rope without letting go of either end.

While he is trying to tie a knot, stand with your arms folded. When he gives up, ask him to hand the rope to you. Take the ends of the rope in your hands without unfolding your arms. Unfold your arms, and there will be a knot in the rope!

STRING IN THE STRAW

THE TRICK

Thread a string through a straw, cut through the straw with scissors, and hold up the string—uncut!

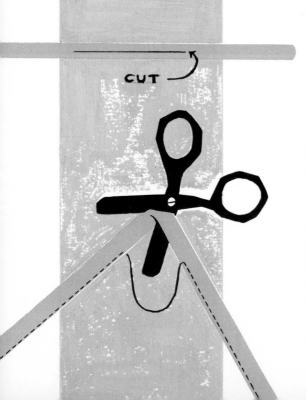

HOW YOU DO IT

Beforehand, cut a slit about two inches long in the center of the straw. Thread the string through the straw in front of the audience. Bend the straw in the center, as shown, with the slit on the underside. Then the string will fall through the slit. Hold the straw so that the string is hidden behind your fingers. Cut the straw in two pieces with scissors, and pull out the string.

Hold up the string so everyone can see that it has not been cut.

THE RING THROUGH THE STRING

THE TRICK

Announce that you can pass a ring through a string while the string is held by two persons. Tell everyone to watch closely.

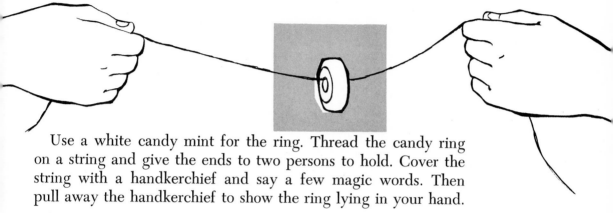

Use a white candy mint for the ring. Thread the candy ring on a string and give the ends to two persons to hold. Cover the string with a handkerchief and say a few magic words. Then pull away the handkerchief to show the ring lying in your hand.

HOW YOU DO IT

You will need to practice this trick a few times before showing it.

The secret of this trick is to have two rings. Before you show the trick, break one ring in two. Wet the broken edges and hold them together until they dry. Then the ring won't crack noisily when you break it. Place this ring on the top of the candy package. Put a handkerchief and the extra mint ring in your pocket.

During the trick, take the mended ring out of the package and thread it on the string. Bring the handkerchief and the extra candy ring out of your pocket at the same time. Spread the handkerchief over the string, keeping your hand closed on the extra ring.

Reach under the handkerchief with both hands. See Picture. Break the mended candy in two, and close your hand over the pieces. Have the extra ring in the other hand. Bring out the hand with the broken pieces in it to take off the handkerchief. See Picture. While everyone is looking at the unbroken ring, put the handkerchief and the pieces in your pocket. Be sure to push the broken pieces to the bottom of your pocket in case anyone wants to look at the handkerchief. Then when you pull out the handkerchief, the pieces won't fall out.

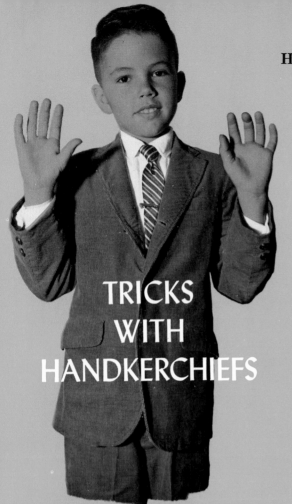

TRICKS WITH HANDKERCHIEFS

HANDKERCHIEF FROM NOWHERE

THE TRICK

Amaze the audience by making a silk handkerchief appear from nowhere.

HOW YOU DO IT

Be sure to wear a suit or a jacket. Roll up a handkerchief as tightly as you can, and hide it in the fold of your coat at the right elbow. Keep this arm slightly bent so the handkerchief won't fall out.

Begin the trick by holding up your hands to the audience to show that they are empty. Push up your sleeves to show that there is nothing hidden in them. Push up the left sleeve first. When you push up the right sleeve, slip the handkerchief from its hiding place into your left hand. Rub your hands together several times, and then let the handkerchief fall from between them.

HANDKERCHIEF KNOT

THE TRICK

Make a handkerchief knot itself—right before everyone's eyes.

HOW YOU DO IT

The secret is to knot one corner of a handkerchief ahead of time.

Ask one of your friends for a handkerchief, but before he can give you one, find your own in your pocket.

This will make your friends think any handkerchief will do.

Hold both ends of the handkerchief in one hand. Flip your hand up and down and pretend to make a knot appear. Hold the knotted corner in your hand and let the other end drop. Look disappointed when no knot appears. On the third flip, let go of the knotted corner, holding the other end with your fingers.

164

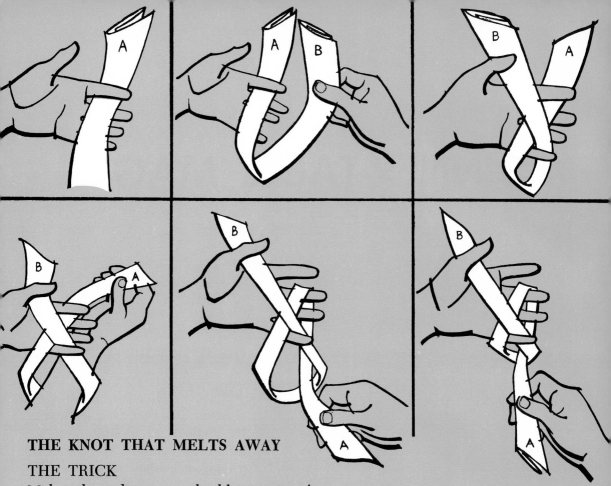

THE KNOT THAT MELTS AWAY

THE TRICK

Make a knot disappear—by blowing on it!

HOW YOU DO IT

The secret is in the way you tie the knot. Follow the pictures.

1. Take one end of the handkerchief between the first and second fingers of your left hand. This is End A.

2. Bring up End B with your right hand.

3. Place End B between your left thumb and first finger.

4. With your right hand reach through the loop that hangs down and take End A between your fingers.

5. Pull this end back through the loop. Keep a tight hold on the handkerchief with your second and third fingers.

6. Pull End A toward you to tighten knot.

7. Slip your fingers out of the knot. Do not pull any more on the knot. Hold the handkerchief by both ends and blow on it. At the same time pull on the ends. The knot vanishes!

DINNER-TABLE MAGIC

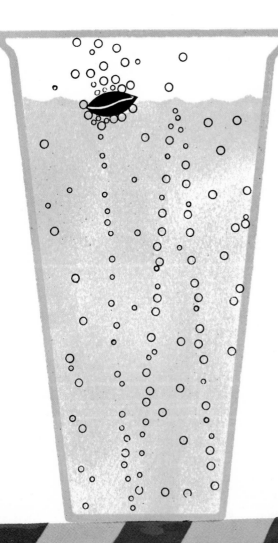

THE MYSTERIOUS FRUIT SEED

THE TRICK

Announce that you are going to "hypnotize" a fruit seed to follow your orders. Tell the seed to rise in a glass of ginger ale, and it rises. Tell it to sink, and it goes to the bottom.

HOW YOU DO IT

Drop an apple or a grape seed into a glass of ginger ale or soda water. The seed first sinks because of its weight. Then it rises when soda bubbles form on it. When it comes to the top of the glass, the bubbles burst, and it sinks again. Then more bubbles form around the seed, and it rises again.

Try this trick beforehand so you will know how long it takes for the seed to rise and sink.

THE TRICK

Pretend to make a coin disappear, but make a salt shaker disappear instead!

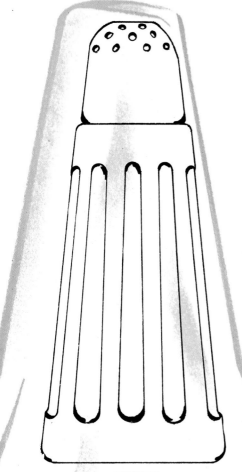

HOW YOU DO IT

Lay a coin on the table, and place a salt shaker over it. Cover the shaker with a paper napkin. Announce that you are going to knock the coin through the table.

Hold the napkin around the salt shaker and tap the top of it. Then lift the shaker—the coin is still there. Set the shaker back over the coin, and tap again. The napkin falls flat. The salt shaker is gone!

The success of this trick depends on making everyone think the coin is going to disappear. They will watch the coin, not the shaker.

When you place the napkin over the salt shaker, crush it down tightly so that it takes the shape of the shaker. After the first tap, lift the shaker and lean forward to look at the coin. At the same time, bring the shaker toward the edge of the table. Touch the coin with your left hand while you let the shaker fall out of your right hand into your lap. Then replace the napkin on the table carefully so it still keeps the shape of the salt shaker. Tap the shaker for the second time, and it falls flat.

Pretend to be as puzzled as everyone else. Shake the napkin and look around for the salt shaker. Have everyone look for the shaker before you finally set it on the table.

Practice this trick a few times beforehand so you can do it easily.

TRICKS

Pick a Penny

THE TRICK

Pick a marked penny from a group of pennies in a hat without looking.

HOW YOU DO IT

Borrow a penny from one of your friends and mark it with a pencil so everyone will recognize it. Ask someone to hold the penny in his hand to "magnetize" it. Then drop the penny into a hat or a box with four or five other pennies.

Reach into the hat or box and remove the pennies one at a time without looking at them. You will be able to tell the "magnetized" penny at once because it will be warm from being held in the person's hand.

WITH COINS

The Magic Eye

THE TRICK

Announce to your friends that you can "see" the date on a coin—even though it is covered with paper.

HOW YOU DO IT

Ask someone to place a coin face up on the table and cover it with a paper. Rub a pencil back and forth across the coin. The date will show plainly.

Double Your Money

THE TRICK

Rub a penny in your hand and suddenly—two pennies appear!

HOW YOU DO IT

The secret is to have two pennies before you begin the trick. Start by reaching into your pocket with your right hand and removing the pennies. Hold one between your thumb and second finger and hide the other between your first and second fingers. See Picture 1.

Show your friends the penny between your thumb and second finger by tossing it back and forth in your palm. See Picture 2.

Now tell your friends that the magic penny will soon multiply into two pennies. Lay it on the palm of your left hand and rub it a few times with your right hand. As you rub, let the second penny drop from between your fingers into your palm. Open your hand to show the two pennies. See Picture 3.

Practice this trick a few times before you show it.

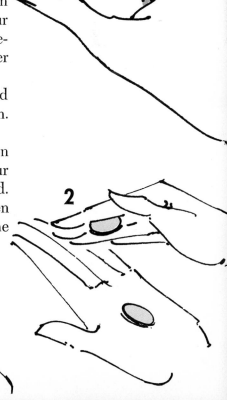

tricks with cards

TAKE A CARD

THE TRICK

A friend chooses a card from the deck, but does not show it to you before he puts it back. You shuffle the cards and then pull his card out of the deck, much to his surprise.

HOW YOU DO IT

Let a friend pick a card from the deck. Tell him to remember what card it was, but not to show it to you.

While he is looking at his card, quickly glance at the bottom card of the deck.

Now have him put his card on top of the deck. Take the card from the bottom and place it on top of his card.

Shuffle the cards as many times as you wish, but always shuffle so the two top cards remain on top of the deck. You will be able to do this easily with practice.

Now divide the deck in two parts, and put the bottom part on top of the deck.

You can now go through the deck, card by card, to find his card. You will know his card when you reach it because it will be right after your card.

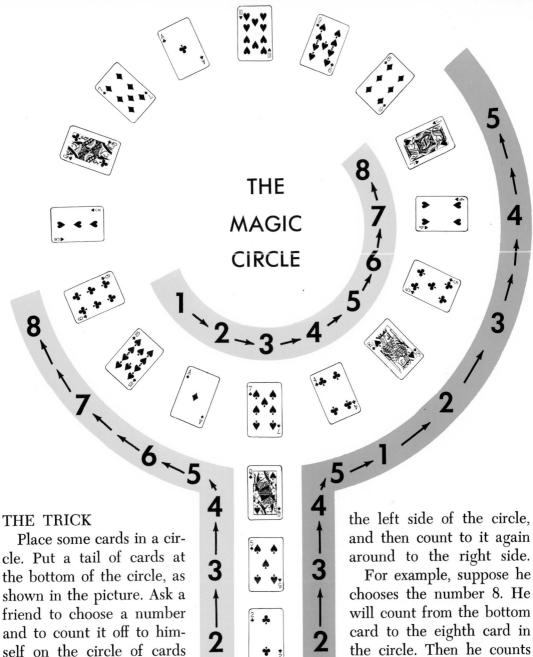

THE
MAGIC
CIRCLE

THE TRICK

Place some cards in a circle. Put a tail of cards at the bottom of the circle, as shown in the picture. Ask a friend to choose a number and to count it off to himself on the circle of cards just the way you tell him. When he is through, surprise him by telling him which card he counted last.

HOW YOU DO IT

The secret is that no matter what number he uses he will always land on the same card. He should first count to his number around the left side of the circle, and then count to it again around to the right side.

For example, suppose he chooses the number 8. He will count from the bottom card to the eighth card in the circle. Then he counts back to the right until he comes to the eighth card.

To find the card his number will fall on, you simply count to yourself the number of cards in the tail under the circle, and then count the same number of cards inside the circle to the right. Both of you will stop on the same card.

TRICKS

AH!
you are
10 years
old!

BIRTHDAY MAGIC

THE TRICK

Here's a way to find out the month of a person's birthday and his age.

HOW YOU DO IT

Give a friend a piece of paper and tell him not to let you see what he writes except for the final answer.

Ask him to write the number of the month of his birthday, such as 1 for January, 2 for February, 3 for March, and so on up to 12 for December. Then ask him to multiply the number of his birth month by 2 and add 5 to his answer. Next have him multiply his last answer by 50, and add his age. To this total have him add 115, and subtract 365 (the number of days in a year). He is to tell you his answer. The first number will be the month of his birthday and the last will be his age.

For example, a person who is 10 years old and whose birthday is in March would do this:

Multiply 3 (for March) by 2	6
Add 5	+5
	11
Multiply by 50	×50
	550
Add his age (10)	+10
	560
Add 115	+115
	675
Subtract 365	−365
	310
3-month, 10-age	

WITH NUMBERS

THE PREDICTED ANSWER

Write the number 1089 on a piece of paper and give it to a friend to hold. Then ask him to write a three-figure number with each figure different, such as 421. Under this number ask him to write the same number backwards—124. Now ask him to subtract the smaller number from the larger one (421 124). Then ask him to turn the answer backwards and add this number to the answer (297+792).

He will be surprised to find that the answer is 1089, the number on the paper he is holding.

Here are some examples:

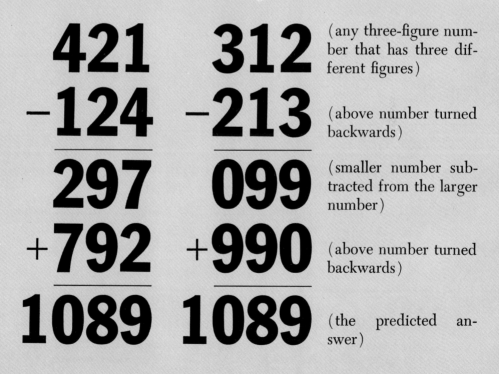

421	(any three-figure number that has three different figures)
−124	(above number turned backwards)
297	(smaller number subtracted from the larger number)
+792	(above number turned backwards)
1089	(the predicted answer)

312	
−213	
099	
+990	
1089	

If your answer (like the 99 above) should have only two figures, add a zero to make three figures (099).

ghost writing

THE TRICK

Tell your friends that you can make writing mysteriously appear between two pieces of cardboard that are tied together.

HOW YOU DO IT

1. Place two pieces of cardboard, a black crayon, and some string on a table. Have everyone examine the cardboard pieces to see that there is no writing.

2. Tie the two pieces together. Place the cardboard package and crayon on the table. Turn out the lights.

3. Quietly pick up the crayon and write a message on the top card, such as "Guess who?" or "Boo!" Then turn the cards over so the message is face down. Ask someone to turn on the lights.

4. Untie the string, being careful not to let anyone turn over the cards. Everyone will expect the writing to be on the inside of the cardboard, so open the cards like a book. Look disappointed because there is no writing, and suggest that you be allowed to try again.

5. Tie the cardboard pieces together again, making sure that the card you wrote on is on top of the other card. Ask everyone to write his initials on the outside card to show that the cards aren't switched.

6. After a minute, turn on the lights, and ask someone to open the cardboard package. Your friends will be surprised to see the ghost writing on the inside.

shows and costumes

Be a clown, or a pirate, or a gypsy, and then put on a show. Let's make believe! The shows and costumes on the next pages will give you some good ideas for dressing up and acting.

Outdoor Hobby Fair

A hobby fair will give you and your friends an opportunity to show off your hobbies. It may also help you to learn new ones. You can have the fair in your back yard—or in any empty lot.

PAINTINGS AND DRAWINGS

COLLECTIONS OF ALL KINDS

MODEL AIRPLANES

RECORDS

PETS

FLOWERS

CLAY MODELS
AND MOSAICS

177

PHOTOGRAPHY

A STAGE SHOW

A stage show is fun for those who act out the story as well as for those who watch the show. After a practice or two, the show will be ready to put on.

The Story
You can make up the story yourself. Or act out a favorite story, a comic strip, or a show you have seen on television. You can even act out one of your story records.

The Actors
Anyone can play a part in a show. Try to speak clearly so that the audience can hear. Be sure to know the story so that you and the other actors know what to do next.

The Stage
Your stage can be a porch, a basement, a corner or end of a room, or part of a back yard. The actors might use a door to come on and off the stage.

The Scenery

The scenery for a play need not look real. Use just enough scenery to let the audience know where the story is taking place.

Paint your scenery on pieces of wrapping paper and stretch them across the back of the stage. You can also use on-stage scenery such as tables and chairs.

The Costumes

You don't have to have fancy costumes to put on a show. The right kind of hat or cape, or simply a cane or a handbag, is usually all you need to get your audience to imagine the rest of the costume.

SOUND EFFECTS

Sound effects make a show seem more exciting. Ask someone to be the "sound man" during the show. Here are some sound effects for him to make: Roll stones in a cigar box to sound like rain, beat a drum to sound like thunder, squeeze a box of cornstarch to sound like someone walking in snow, crumple paper to sound like a fire burning, and pat hands on a table to sound like horses running.

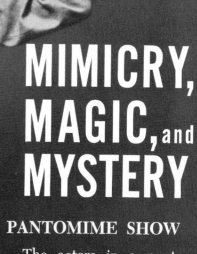

MARCEL MARCEAU

MIMICRY, MAGIC, and MYSTERY

PANTOMIME SHOW

The actors in a pantomime show do not talk. They act out a story with hand, face, and body movements.

You can make a whole pantomime show about a little old man who has lost something. Have the actor look through his pockets, inside his hat, around the room—even on the floor under the seats of the people watching the show.

Or have a show with someone acting out a funny story without using words. You might play records during the show and have the actor pretend to be singing or telling the story.

SHADOW SHOW

You can have a shadow show if you use a sheet and a bright lamp. Have someone hang the sheet over a doorway. Place the lamp behind the sheet. See Picture.

When the actors move around between the sheet and the light, their shadows show on the sheet. Someone might tell a story or play a record during the show. The actors can wear hats that make different-shaped shadows on the sheet.

MAGIC SHOW

If you know some magic tricks, you can put on a magic show for your friends. You will find some magic tricks on pages 158 to 174.

VARIETY SHOW

Everyone can have an act in a variety show. And it can be almost any kind of act. Someone can sing a song. Someone else can do a tap dance.

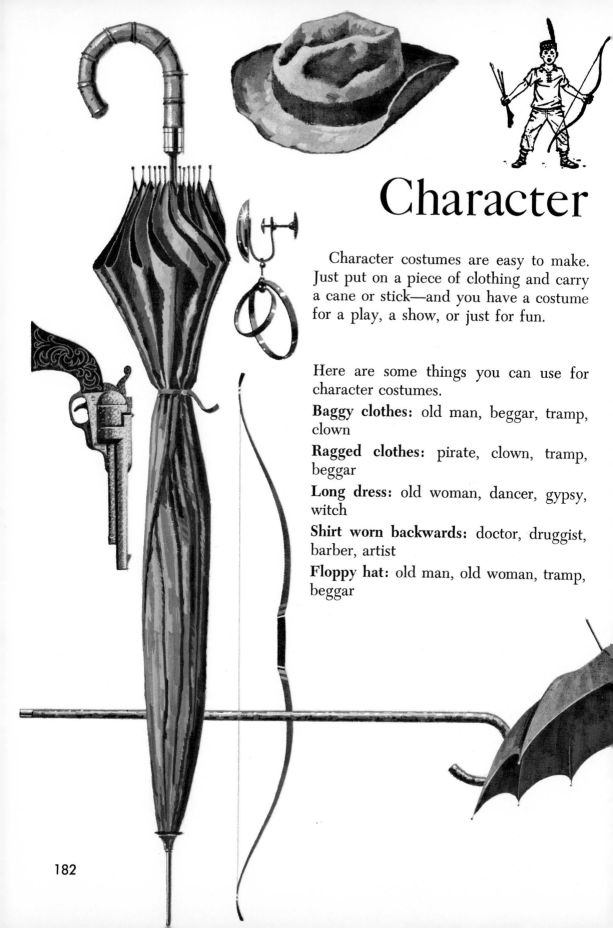

Character

Character costumes are easy to make. Just put on a piece of clothing and carry a cane or stick—and you have a costume for a play, a show, or just for fun.

Here are some things you can use for character costumes.

Baggy clothes: old man, beggar, tramp, clown

Ragged clothes: pirate, clown, tramp, beggar

Long dress: old woman, dancer, gypsy, witch

Shirt worn backwards: doctor, druggist, barber, artist

Floppy hat: old man, old woman, tramp, beggar

Costumes

Saucepan on head: soldier, knight, space-man

Straw hat: farmer, country boy, country girl

Scarf: old woman, gypsy, cowboy, farmer, pirate

Towel cape: Robin Hood, knight

Crepe-paper cape: queen, fairy princess

Umbrella: old man, old woman, clown

Cane: old man, old woman, beggar

Toy pistol: cowboy, pirate, soldier, spaceman

Bow and arrows: Robin Hood, Indian

Hoop earrings: pirate, gypsy

Lipstick: Indian warpaint, clown make-up

Cotton for beard or hair: old man, tramp, beggar

COSTUMES

Ringmaster
Materials
• 2 pieces of cardboard • tape • black paint • black crepe paper • string and a stick for the whip

For the ringmaster's hat, make a tube out of cardboard wide enough to fit around your head. Tape the ends together.

Stand the tube on another piece of cardboard and draw around it to make a circle. Draw another larger circle around the first one.

Cut out each circle. Tape the small circle to one end of the tube for the top of the hat. Then tape the large circle to the other end for a brim.

Cut a bow tie out of black crepe paper.

Band Costume
Materials
• red crepe paper • cardboard • construction paper • tape

Cut three strips, each about as wide as your hand, from an unopened package of crepe paper.

Pin two of the strips, crisscrossed, to your blouse or shirt. Save the other strip.

Make a tube out of construction paper for the hat. It should be large enough to fit on your head. Tape the ends together.

For the feather, cut a piece of cardboard about two fingers wide and a little longer than the hat. Cut slits along the edge of your third crepe-paper strip. Wrap the strip around the cardboard.

CIRCUS
ANIMAL
COSTUMES

Animal Heads and Tails

You and your friends can dress to look like lions, tigers, and elephants. Wear leotards, pajamas, or coveralls, and put on animal heads and tails made from paper bags.

Materials
- large paper bags   • construction paper
- crepe paper   • tape   • glue   • ribbon
- rope   • black paint   • wrapping paper

Find a paper bag large enough to fit over your head. Cut out a heart shape in front for your face. See Picture.

Cut animal ears out of construction paper and glue them to the corners of the bag.

Cut strips of paper for whiskers. Glue them in place.

Make the tail by wrapping crepe paper around a piece of clothesline. Pin the tail to the back of your clothes.

A lion's mane can be made by pasting strips of wrapping paper around the sides and back of the paper head.

To make a tiger's head, paint black stripes on the bag.

Make an elephant's trunk by wrapping crepe paper around the thick rope. Or cut two long crepe paper strips, about twice as wide as you want the trunk to be. Glue the sides and ends together, leaving one end open to stuff with cut-up pieces of paper. Glue the trunk to the bag. Cut tusks out of cardboard. Add big floppy elephant ears cut out of construction paper.

CLOWN COSTUMES

In just a few minutes you can make yourself look like a circus clown.

Ask if you can use a pair of your father's old pajamas and a pair of his old shoes. Put on the pajamas and step into the shoes. If someone ties strings around the bottom of the pajama pants, you will look more like a clown. Now you're ready to make up your face to look like a clown.

Materials
- stocking (an old, white work sock is best)
- bits of yarn for hair • string • cold cream • flour or bath powder • lipstick and eyebrow pencil • cork

MAKE A STOCKING CAP TO COVER YOUR HAIR

Cut off the top of an old, white stocking. Tie a string around the cut end. Turn it inside out. Glue, staple, or sew bits of yarn to the stocking cap for hair. Put on the cap and tuck in your hair.

WHITE-FACED CLOWN

Ask mother for some cold cream and an old lipstick and eyebrow pencil.

Cover your face, neck, and ears with cold cream. Wipe off any extra cream. Pat on flour or bath powder.

Draw eyebrows, long eyelashes, a wide mouth, and red cheeks with the lipstick and the eyebrow pencil.

Mold a ball of clay for a nose.

DIRTY-FACED CLOWN

You can dress as a tramp clown, too. Put on ragged or patched old clothes. Ask your mother to help you burn the end of a cork to mark up your face. When the cork cools, rub it over your face. Then draw other parts of the face with lipstick.

When you want to stop being a clown, use cold cream to take off your make-up.

CLOWNING

Clowns do all kinds of silly things to make people laugh. They tumble, trip, fall, slip, and slide in their big shoes and baggy clothes. They do funny dances and chase each other around the ring. Sometimes clowns play tricks on one another to get laughs.

HALLOWEEN

GHOST

Ask your mother for an old sheet or a tablecloth.

Cut two round holes for eyes, and your costume is ready to wear.

A WITCH HAT

Materials
- 2 pieces of cardboard or 2 large sheets of construction paper
- black poster paint • tape

Cut out a large circle from cardboard. The larger the circle, the higher the hat will be. Cut a slit up to the middle of the circle, as in the picture. Shape the circle into a cone, and tape the ends together.

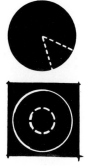

Place the bottom of the cone on another piece of cardboard and trace around it. Then draw a larger circle around the first one. See Picture. Cut out the circles, and you have a brim for the hat. Tape the brim to the bottom of the cone.

Paint the hat with black poster paint.

COSTUMES

A BLACK CAT

Materials

• paper bag • black poster paint • pipe cleaners • black construction paper • black crepe paper • clothesline

Use a paper bag large enough to fit over your head. Paint it black.

Cut holes in the bag for the eyes.

Cut pointed ears from construction paper and glue them to the bag.

Punch holes in front of the bag and stick pipe cleaners through them to make whiskers. Tape the pipe cleaners in place.

Make the tail by wrapping crepe paper around a piece of clothesline. Pin the tail to the back of your clothes.

HALLOWEEN MASK

Materials

• construction paper, cardboard, or crepe paper • string or cord

Fold a sheet of construction paper in half. Draw a half circle on the paper, as in the picture.

Cut around the circle. Then cut an eyehole in the folded mask Punch a hole near the edge for the string.

Unfold the mask. Tie string through the holes. Or staple the ends of a long rubber band to the mask.

Decorate the mask with poster paints and bits of construction paper.

DRESS-UP COSTUMES

It's fun to dress up in mother's or dad's old clothes.

You can dress up as an old man, an old woman, a clown, a tramp, a pirate, an Indian, or a cowboy, depending on the clothes you have. The pictures on this page will give you some ideas.

Choose old clothes like these:

suits	shoes	belts	robes	gloves
pajamas	handbags	neckties	dresses	hats
gowns	umbrellas	jewelry	coats	scarfs

puppets and marionettes

Wood, cloth, paper, and even sawdust can be turned into a puppet—a doll that fits over your hand, or a marionette—a doll that is fastened to strings. You will find many easy-to-make puppets and marionettes on the next pages.

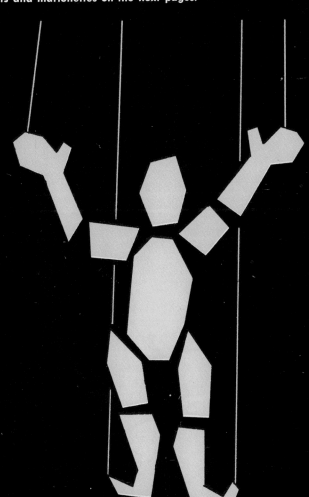

STICK PUPPETS

Materials
- cardboard • paste • tape
- magazine pictures of people standing up
- ruler for each puppet or other strips of wood about the size of a ruler

Cut out magazine pictures of people standing. Paste the pictures on cardboard and then cut out the figures.

Tape each picture, standing up, to an old ruler or strip of wood, as shown.

Use a box or a table for the puppet stage. Hold the end of the ruler, and move the puppet around on the stage.

Hang a sheet over the stage to hide you. The audience is supposed to watch the puppets, not you.

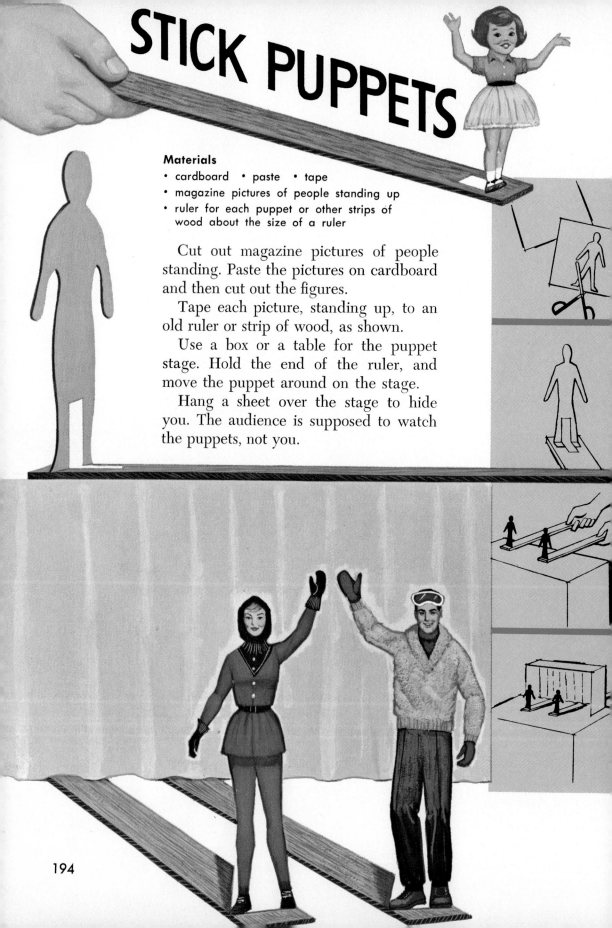

Finger Puppets

Materials
- an old glove
- cardboard
- crayons
- glue

On a piece of cardboard, draw the body, the head, and the arms of the puppet actor you want. Do not draw any legs.

Color your drawing. Cut it out, and glue it to the back of an old glove, just above the second finger of the glove. See Picture.

Put the glove over your hand. Your first and second fingers will be the legs of the puppet. You can make the puppet walk, dance, run, and sit down by moving your fingers.

FIST PUPPET

Make a fist with your thumb tucked under your fingers. Your fist will be the puppet's head. Your thumb will be the puppet's mouth. Move your thumb up, down, and sideways to make the puppet look as if it were talking.

Use an eyebrow pencil to draw eyes and a nose on your fist head. Outline the mouth with lipstick. See Picture.

You can attach crepe-paper ears and a collar to your fist with paste. When you are through with your fist puppet, rub off the paste and wash away the lipstick and eyebrow pencil marks.

Materials
- lipstick
- eyebrow pencil
- crepe paper
- paste

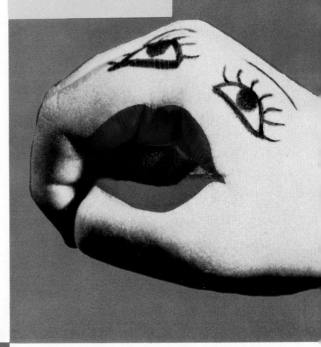

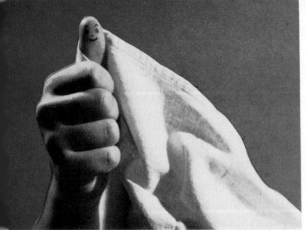

THUMBELLINA

Draw a face on your thumb with an eyebrow pencil. Wrap a handkerchief around your thumb, as shown in the picture. Now your puppet will move when you wiggle your thumb.

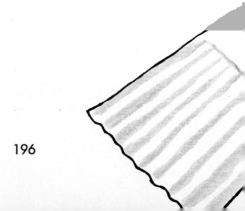

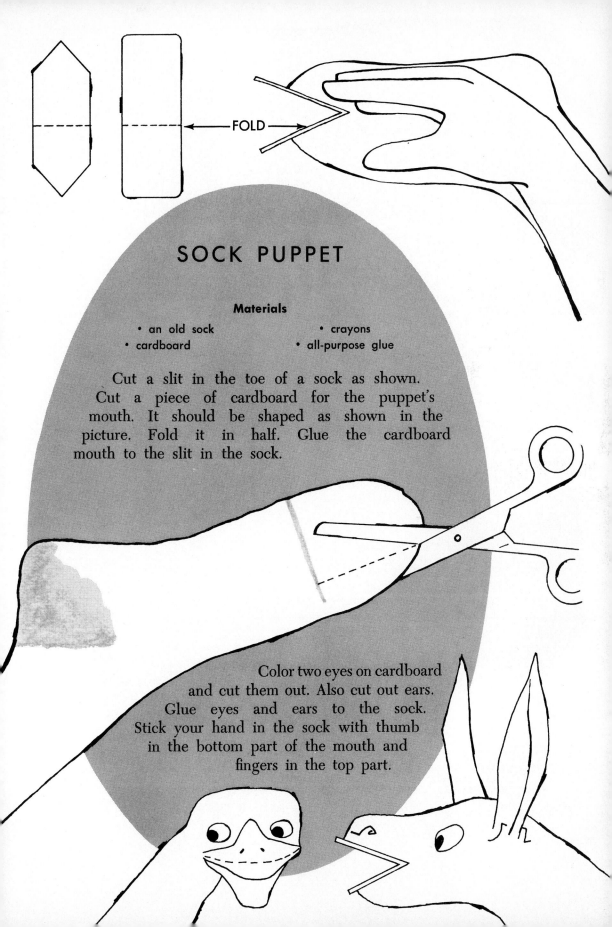

FOLD

SOCK PUPPET

Materials

- an old sock
- cardboard
- crayons
- all-purpose glue

Cut a slit in the toe of a sock as shown. Cut a piece of cardboard for the puppet's mouth. It should be shaped as shown in the picture. Fold it in half. Glue the cardboard mouth to the slit in the sock.

Color two eyes on cardboard and cut them out. Also cut out ears. Glue eyes and ears to the sock. Stick your hand in the sock with thumb in the bottom part of the mouth and fingers in the top part.

Paper Bag PUPPETS

Materials

• a small brown paper bag
for each puppet • paste • string
• yarn, cotton, or crepe paper
for hair • crayons
• old newspapers

Lay a paper bag flat on the table with the bottom away from you. Draw a face on the upper half of the bag. See Pictures. Stuff the bag half full of crumpled pieces of newspaper.

Stick your hand into the bag, pushing your first finger into the newspaper stuffing.

Your thumb and second finger are to be the arms of the puppet. Punch out or cut holes where your fingers should stick through.

Paste hair made of yarn, cotton, or crepe-paper strips on the bag.

Tie a string around the bag, just below the face and above the armholes.

Two-Bag Puppets

Two-bag puppets are made in much the same way that you make paper-bag puppets. But use one bag for the head and one for the body. Stuff the head bag with crumpled paper, and tie a string around the open end for a neck.

Cut three holes in the other bag—one at each corner for your fingers, and one in the center for the neck from the other bag. See Picture.

Stuff the neck in the center hole.

199

Materials

- sawdust
- wallpaper paste
- water
- an empty pop bottle
- sandpaper
- tempera paints
- shellac
- cloth scraps
- Styrofoam

Sawdust Puppet Head

Styrofoam Puppet Head

Cloth Puppet Head

200

One cup of sawdust from any lumberyard is enough to make a puppet head. Mix enough water with the sawdust to make it pack like wet sand. Add dry wallpaper paste and a little more water to make a mixture that feels like clay.

Wrap a scrap of cloth around the neck of a pop bottle. Stick a lump of the sawdust clay over the cloth on the neck of the bottle, and mold it into a head. Let the head dry. After it is dry, take it off the bottle and smooth it down with sandpaper.

Paint the head with tempera. After the paint dries, cover it with shellac.

A Styrofoam ball can be used for a puppet head. Buy a Styrofoam ball at a dime store. You can dent and cut Styrofoam, stick pins in it, and paste things on it.

Use the handle of a spoon to punch a finger hole in the bottom of the ball of Styrofoam. See Picture.

Push pieces of cardboard into the Styrofoam for a nose and for ears. They can also be attached with straight pins. Paste yarn in place for hair. Cut out pieces of paper or cloth for the eyes and the mouth. Paste these in place.

Cut the toe off an old sock to make a cloth puppet head. Stuff it with cotton.

Wrap cardboard around your middle finger to make a tube. Glue or tape it in place. Be sure it is wrapped loosely enough so that you can slip your finger in and out easily.

Tie the open end of the sock around the cardboard tube. See Picture.

Sew a puppet face on the head. Use pieces of felt, cloth scraps, buttons, yarn, or thread.

201

Puppet and Marionette

Puppet and marionette stages are made so that the audience can see the puppets and the marionettes in a show without seeing you, the puppeteer, managing them.

Puppets are worked from below a stage. Marionettes are worked by strings from above the stage. So a marionette stage does not have to be as high off the floor as a puppet stage.

CARD-TABLE PUPPET STAGE

Turn a card table on its side. You can crouch behind the table, and reach up above the edge of it to work the puppets.

CURTAIN PUPPET STAGE

Tack a curtain or a large piece of crepe paper across the bottom of a doorway. Hide behind the curtain and hold up the puppets. You can also fasten the curtain between two chairs.

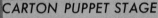

CARTON PUPPET STAGE

Cut a window in a large cardboard carton. See Picture. Hide behind the carton, and hold the puppets up to the window. Use poster paints to decorate the carton.

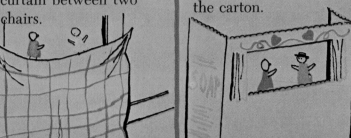

Stages

MARIONETTE STAGES

Marionette stages have two parts—the backdrop and the frontdrop. The backdrop hides your legs when you work the marionettes. The frontdrop hides the upper part of your body.

Make the backdrop out of a sheet of cardboard. You can paint scenery on one side of it. Brace it with something at each end to keep it from falling over.

Set the backdrop on the floor, on a sturdy table strong enough to stand on, or on some wooden crates. Then stand behind the backdrop when you work the marionettes.

To make the frontdrop, hang a sheet or a curtain several feet in front of the backdrop. It should be high enough so that it does not cover the backdrop.

CARDBOARD MARIONETTE

Materials
- heavy cardboard
- paper fasteners
- string
- crayons

Draw a boy or a girl without arms on cardboard. Draw two separate arms. Color the boy or the girl and the arms as you wish, and cut them out.

Make a small hole in each shoulder. Make a small hole at the shoulder end of each arm. Attach the arms to the shoulders with paper fasteners. Be sure that the arms move easily after the fasteners are in place.

Attach a string to the top of the head. Attach strings to each hand.

Tie the other end of the string from the cardboard marionette's head to your own wrist. Tie one of the strings from the marionette's hand to your thumb, and the other to one of your fingers.

Now, as you move your arm, the marionette will move across the stage. As you move your fingers, the arms of the marionette will wave.

204

Marionettes

CEREAL-CARTON MARIONETTE

Materials

- a regular-size cereal carton
- a single-portion cereal carton
- cardboard
- string
- tempera paints
- a piece of clothesline
- tape

Poke a hole in the top of a regular-size cereal carton. This hole is for the marionette's neck. Poke two holes in the bottom of the carton for the legs and a hole in each side for the arms.

Cut two pieces of clothesline for the legs, two pieces for the arms, and another piece for the neck. All of these pieces should be about the same length. Tie a knot at the end of each piece. Open the ends of the box and push a piece of clothesline through each hole from the inside, all the way up to the knot. Close the box ends and tape them shut.

Poke a hole in the end of a small single-portion cereal carton for the marionette's neck. Push the other end of the rope that is the neck piece through the hole in the small box. Tie a knot to fasten it in the box. Tape the box shut.

Cut two hands and two feet out of cardboard and tape them to the ends of the arms and the legs. Paint the marionette with tempera paints.

Attach one string to the top of the marionette's head and one string to each of the marionette's hands. Tie the head string to your wrist, and the hand string to your fingers.

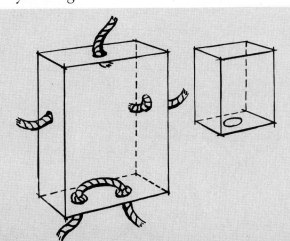

PAPIER-MÂCHÉ BALLOON MARIONETTES

Use a large balloon for the head and a small one for the body. Cover both balloons with papier-mâché strips in the way shown on page 92.

Bend pieces of wire to make arms and legs, as shown. Cover the wires with papier-mâché strips.

Use tape to attach the head, arms, and legs loosely to the body.

Add cardboard ears. Paint on the eyes, the nose, and the mouth.

Attach strings to the head, the hands, and the feet. Tie the strings to a pencil or an ice-cream stick control. Pull on the leg string to make the leg move, on the arm string to make the arm move.

Use five round balloons for the worm. Cover them with papier-mâché strips in the way shown on page 92.

Paint the paper-covered balloons with tempera paints.

Use tape to join the balloons, but leave enough room between the balloons to let the worm wiggle.

Attach strings along the back of the worm, one for each balloon. Tie the other end of each string to a pencil or ice-cream stick control.

ARM WIRE   LEG WIRE

DWARF

WIGGLY WORM

206

needle and thread

Make an apron, make a clown, or make a pair of slippers to wear
around. Or you can stitch a picture or braid a belt as a gift for a
friend. All you need are needle, thread and a few other materials.
It's easy. Follow the steps closely on the next pages and see.

PICTURES

made of thread

Making Pictures with Stitches

Draw a picture of a boat, a cat, a house, a boy, or a girl on paper. With carbon paper under your drawing, trace the lines onto the cloth.

Thread a big needle. Double the thread and make a knot at the end.

Now you're ready to sew along the lines. Start by sticking the needle through the backside of the cloth and pulling the thread through until the knot stops it. Push the needle in and out of the cloth along the lines of the picture until you have covered all of the lines. Sew short, tight stitches.

Sewing Pictures on Cards

Stitch pictures on cardboard instead of on cloth, and you can make a collection of card pictures.

Use a thimble when you push the needle through the cardboard.

Beanbag

You can make a beanbag out of the picture you stitched in cloth. Cut another piece of cloth the same size as your cloth picture.

Place the cloth picture face down on the other piece of cloth.

Sew around three sides with two rows of short, tight stitches so that the beans can't spill out. Leave one side open so that you can put in beans or rice.

Turn the bag inside out. Now the stitched edges are inside, and the picture shows on the outside.

Fill the bag with beans or rice through the open end.

Sew up the open end, using the overhand stitch. Make the stitches close together, so the beans won't spill out.

Materials
- a piece of soft cloth
  (use old sheet or muslin
  or piece of thin cardboard)
- a needle
- embroidery thread, or yarn
- paper • carbon paper

Sewing Cloth Picture on Cloth

Cut out shapes of houses, trees, flowers, or animals from scraps of brightly colored cloth. Place the cutout shapes on another piece of cloth and arrange them to make a picture.

Pin the pieces to the cloth. Sew around the pieces, using an overhand stitch. See Picture. This kind of sewing is called "appliqué." (ap-li-kay)

ASK FOR HELP

Materials
- a cotton dish towel
  or
- a terry-cloth towel
- ribbon for tying
- a needle and thread
- crayons

aprons for

BARBECUE APRON

Use a dish towel or a terry-cloth towel that your mother will let you have. Be sure it is large enough to fit the person you are making the apron for.

Cut the ribbon into two pieces. Sew each piece to a corner of the towel. See Picture. Now you have an apron.

If you use a white dish towel, you can draw a colorful picture on it with crayons. To keep the picture from rubbing off, turn the apron, picture-side down, on a damp cloth. With grown-up help, press with a hot iron.

CHEF

work or *play*

CLOTHESPIN OR CARPENTER'S APRON

You can make an apron for clothespins or a carpenter's apron out of towels, too. Make the pocket for clothespins or nails by turning up the bottom edge of the towel. Sew the turned-up edge to the apron. See Picture.

If you wish, you can make the clothespin pocket into two smaller pockets by sewing a double row of stitches up the front of the fold in the middle. See Picture.

For the carpenter's apron, sew two double rows of stitches to make three pockets—one for big nails, one for small nails, and one for screws.

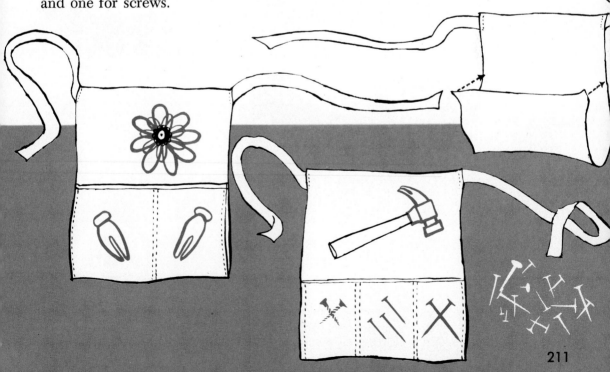

A CLOWN

Draw eyes, nose, and mouth on the clown face. Sew along the lines with embroidery thread or yarn.

Or sew buttons to the face for the eyes and the nose, and draw the mouth with a crayon.

Color the cheeks, the chin, and the forehead with crayon, if you wish.

Materials
- a piece of an old sheet or a soft cotton cloth
- a piece of colored cloth for ruffles
- paper for pattern   • buttons
- cotton for stuffing   • crayons
- yarn for hair and face
- a needle and thread

OUT OF CLOTH

Draw a paper pattern for the
clown body like the one on
this page, but much larger.
Cut it out.
Pin the pattern
to two layers of cloth and
cut around it.
Using a short
stitch, start to sew the
pieces together from
Point A. Stop sewing at B.
This will leave an opening at the top of the head for stuffing.
Look at
the pattern picture.
    Turn the clown body inside out so that the seams are inside.
Stuff the clown with cotton. Pack the stuffing into the arms
and legs by pushing it in carefully with a pencil. Sew up the
opening at the top of the head, using the overhand stitch.

213

Sew short pieces of yarn
on the head for hair. You
can also use strips of cloth
for hair.

For ruffles, cut five strips
of cloth, each about three
inches wide. Fold, and
stitch the edges together.

Pull the thread until the
cloth bunches up. Sew the
ruffles around the clown's
neck, arms, and legs. Sew
buttons in a line down the
clown's front.

A SKATING OUTFIT

CIRCLE SKIRT   Cut out a paper pattern like the one on this page. Make it large enough to fit your doll. Pin the pattern to the felt and cut 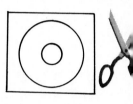 around it.

To make the side opening, cut down from the waist about one-third of the  length of the skirt. See Picture. Sew a piece of ribbon or bias tape to each side of the opening. These will tie around your doll's waist.

SUSPENDERS   Cut two long strips of felt, about as wide as your finger and long enough to reach over your doll's shoulder from the front of the waist to the back. If you wish, add crossbars to the front and back of the suspenders. See Picture. Sew the suspenders to the skirt.

EARWARMER   Cut a strip of felt long enough to cover your doll's head and ears. Cut two strips of bias tape or ribbon long enough to tie under the doll's chin. Sew the strips to the sides of the earwarmer.

MUFF   Cut a square piece of felt. Fold the felt in the middle and sew the top edges of the cloth together. Turn the muff inside out.

FOR A DOLL

Materials
- scrap pieces of felt
- a needle and thread • paper for pattern
- ribbon or bias tape for waist and earwarmer ties

215

MATERIALS
- scrap pieces of cloth
- a needle and thread
- bias tape or ribbon
- a pencil

clothes

You can make a dress
an evening dress,
or a nightgown
for your doll.

DOLL DRESS

Cut a piece of cloth twice as long as you want the dress to be and twice as wide as your doll. Fold the cloth in half, with the wrong side of the cloth facing out. See Picture.

Draw curved lines at the top of the fold. Cut along the lines to make holes for the doll's neck and arms.

Sew up the sides of the dress, using short stitches.

Now turn the dress right side out. Tie a ribbon around the waist, or make a sash from a long strip of cloth.

CLOTH

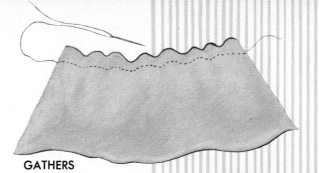

GATHERS

SKIRT

CAPE

SKIRT

SCARF

OR
SHAWL

A

B

HALTER TOP

for your doll

GATHERED SKIRT OR CAPE

With this pattern you can make a gathered skirt, a full petticoat, or a cape.

Cut a long piece of cloth like the one in the picture. Make the cloth bunch up along the top edge by making short stitches and pulling the thread. See Picture. If you want to keep the bottom edge from unraveling, ask your mother to cut it with pinking shears.

Sew the two ends of the piece of cloth together to make the skirt or petticoat.

If you want a cape, make the cloth bunch up to fit around the doll's neck by pulling the thread as tightly as you can. Make a knot to hold it. Sew strings at the top corners for ties on your cape.

SCARF, SHAWL, OR HALTER TOP

Cut out a three-cornered piece of cloth like the one in the picture.

This makes a scarf or a shawl, depending on the size of the cloth.

To make a halter top for your doll to wear with a skirt, fold the top corner down over a long piece of bias tape or ribbon and sew the corner to the scarf. This is the part that goes over the doll's neck. See Picture A. Then sew strips of bias tape or ribbon to the other corners. These tie around the waist. See Picture B.

217

slippers *to wear indoors*

Materials
- scrap pieces of felt
- a piece of old leather, rubber, oilcloth, or terry cloth for slipper soles
- paper for patterns
- a needle and thread
- glue

PAPER PATTERN

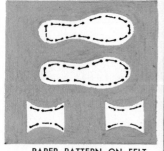

PAPER PATTERN ON FELT

PAPER PATTERN ON
OILCLOTH, RUBBER, LEATHER

Trace around the soles of a pair of shoes to make two paper patterns. Use your shoes or those of a friend. Cut out the patterns. These are for the inside soles and the outside soles. Also cut out a paper pattern for the tops of the slippers. It should be shaped like the one on this page, but it should be large enough to go over the wide part of the sole and let your feet through.

Pin the patterns for the soles and the tops of the slippers to the felt, and cut around the patterns.

Next, pin the patterns for the soles to a piece of leather, rubber, oilcloth, or terry cloth. Cut around the patterns. These pieces will be the outside soles. Glue one outside sole to the matching inside sole of each slipper. Pin the top pieces at the widest part of the soles. Sew or staple them in place.

Decorate the tops as shown on this page.

SEW OR STAPLE TOP PIECE IN PLACE—GLUE SOLES TOGETHER

DECORATE TOPS WITH BOWS, BUTTONS, YARN, OR CLOTH CUTOUTS

218

gifts from cloth squares

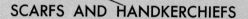

SCARFS AND HANDKERCHIEFS

Cut out a square the size of a headscarf, a neckscarf, or a handkerchief. Make a hem by rolling each edge of the square over the cloth and sewing along the rolled edge. See Picture. Ask your mother to help you with the hem.

The pictures here will give you some ideas for decorating your scarf.

PARTY APRON

Cut out a large square. Sew ribbon around the edge on three sides of the square, or hem the edge. Ask your mother to show you how. Sew a long ribbon along the top for a waistband and strings to tie around your waist. If your mother will let you have four handkerchiefs, you can sew these together for the apron, instead of cutting out a square.

Cut a square from a piece of felt. You can make a coin purse, a cosmetic bag, a clutch bag, or a handbag for your doll, depending on the size of the square.

Fold the cloth as you see in the picture. Sew up the sides of the bag. Fold the top flap over.

BAGS

braided belts and ties

Materials
- a heavy cord or yarn
- tape

A			B				C			D		
1	2	3	1	2	3		1	2	3	1	2	3

Cut three strands of yarn or cord the same length.
Tape or tack one end of each strand to the edge of a
table. The strands should be about the width of a finger apart.

A Bring Strand **3** over Strand **2**.
B Bring Strand **1** over Strand **3**.
C Bring Strand **2** over Strand **1**.

Continue Steps A through C to the end of the strand.
Pull the strand tightly or loosely, depending on how tight or
loose you want the braid to be.
When you are finished, remove the tape and tie knots at
both ends of the braid.
If you wish, you may use two, three, or more pieces of yarn
for each strand to make it thicker. Be sure to divide the
pieces evenly into three strands before you begin braiding.
Once you know how to braid, you can make things like
belts, sashes, neckties, and dog leashes.

220

hiking and camping

Do you like to be outdoors? Do you like to look at the sky? Do you like to walk in the rain or in the snow? Do you like to sleep in a tent and eat food cooked on a campfire? Then you'll enjoy hiking and camping. That's what the next pages are about.

Hiking Hints

You need to know where you're going when you go on a hike. You need a plan. That's why you and your hiking friends should carry a map and a compass. On the map, you can plan the route from home to the place you're hiking to. The compass will help you with directions.

While hiking, you won't tire so quickly if you keep your toes pointed ahead or slightly in. On each step, push off with your toes and put your heel down lightly. Lean a bit forward from the hips, and keep your chin up. Swing your arms naturally.

If you walk so fast that you can't talk, you're racing, not hiking. Slow down.

Every once in a while, you should rest for about five minutes. Then you're on your way again.

You can hurt yourself while hiking if you step on logs that are rotten, or if you step on rocks that are loose or slippery.

Stay as far as possible to the left of any road you may be hiking along. Then you can see approaching cars, and the drivers can see you.

Follow a Track

Make your hike more exciting by tracking an animal. You can track, or follow, an animal by looking for certain kinds of footprints in sand, snow, or places where the ground is damp. If you're quiet and careful, and if you walk against the wind so that the animal can't smell you, the tracks may lead you right to the animal—or to the place where the animal has been. Here are some footprints.

Deer

Otter

Fox

Sheep

Woodchuck

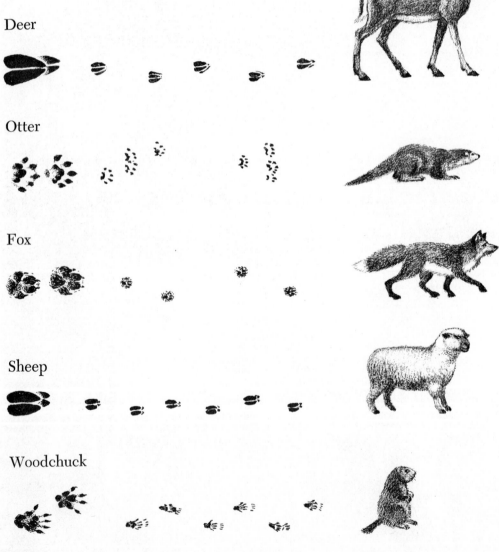

Picking a Campsite

When you go on a hike, watch for a good place to camp. Then, if you ever plan a camping trip in that area later on, you'll already have a place picked to pitch your tent.

The place should be clear of trees and shrubs. Then dead tree branches won't fall on you. And if it rains, raindrops won't keep bothering you, after the rain stops, by dripping on you and your tent.

Look for a place with trees to the west and the north of your campsite. Then you will be able to enjoy more sunlight during the morning. And you'll also be better protected from most of the strong winds.

The campsite should be higher than the area around it. Then you won't be bothered by early morning fog from any nearby lakes. The place should be away from the edge of water. Then you won't be bitten by so many mosquitoes. But make sure there's fresh water close by. Then you will have water to drink and water to bathe with.

Picking a campsite isn't easy—unless it's in a park where there's a camping ground. It's more fun if you find your own campsite.

Follow a Trail

When you go on a hike and follow a trail, you can use some of the trail signs that Indians once used. Of course, you and the person who made the trail have to know what the trail signs mean. For example, if you see a small stone placed on top of a larger stone on the ground, and small stones beside them made like a "V," the trail sign is telling you to go in the direction of the point of the "V."

If you see a small stone placed on top of a larger stone on the ground, with another small stone on the ground and to the right of it, the trail sign is telling you to turn to the right. If the small stone is placed to the left of the two stones that are on top of each other, the trail sign is telling you to turn to the left. And if you see a large stone with a smaller stone on top of it, and an even smaller stone on top of the small stone, this trail sign means, "Watch out for danger!" It may even mean, "Help!"

Things for Camping

Here is a list of things to take with you for camping:

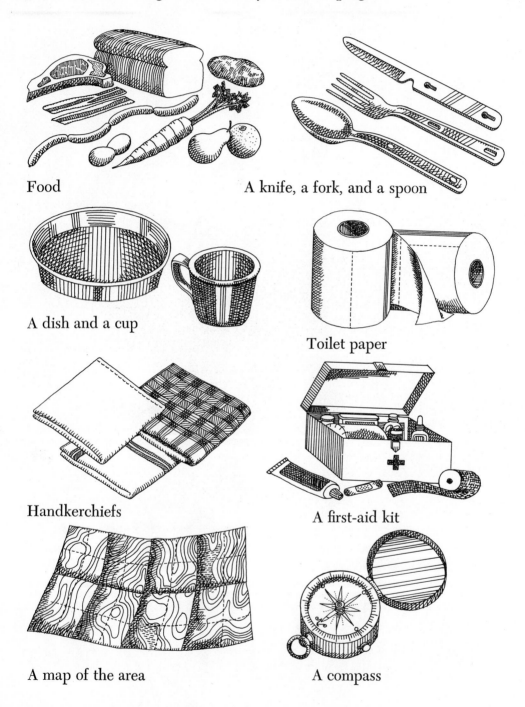

Food

A knife, a fork, and a spoon

A dish and a cup

Toilet paper

Handkerchiefs

A first-aid kit

A map of the area

A compass

A tent

A cot or sleeping bag

Blankets

A plastic or canvas ground cover

A flashlight

A bar of soap

A bath towel

A toothbrush and toothpaste

A comb

A sewing kit

Extra socks, underwear, shirts or blouses

Making a Campfire

You need tinder, kindling, and fuel to make a campfire. Tinder is stuff that lights easily. You can use strips of bark from dead tree branches or from a dead tree stump, or you can use dry leaves and weeds.

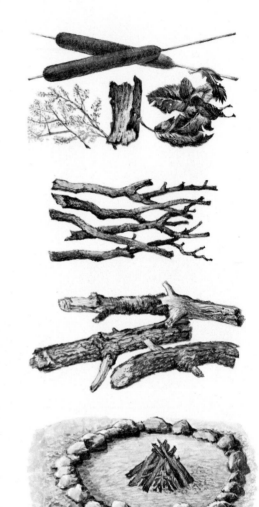

Kindling is the wood that you put on top of the tinder to help make the fire grow stronger. Dead tree branches make good kindling.

Fuel is the wood you place on top of the kindling to keep the fire burning. Find dry sticks on the ground or break dead tree branches into pieces about one foot long.

The safest place to build a campfire is on rock, gravel, or dirt, away from anything like dry grass or leaves that could spread the fire.

To make a small campfire for cooking, make a teepee of kindling over a handful of tinder. Keep your back to the wind, light a match and touch it to the tinder. After the tinder and kindling are burning, start adding thin pieces of fuel. When the thin pieces start to burn, add heavier pieces until the fire is the size you want. Then your campfire is ready to cook something.

Wind ▶

Campfire Cooking

To cook and eat a meal outdoors, you don't need pots, pans, and dishes if you use aluminum foil.

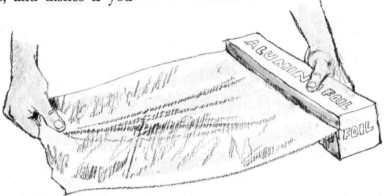

Fold the foil so that it is double. Place the food you want to cook on the foil. Then fold the foil over the food and make a tight package.

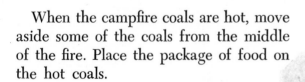

When the campfire coals are hot, move aside some of the coals from the middle of the fire. Place the package of food on the hot coals.

After the food cooks the right amount of time, carefully remove the foil package from the fire. Tear open the foil and eat from it.

One of several meals you can cook in aluminum foil is hamburger with potatoes and carrots. For one serving, use ¼ pound of hamburger to make a patty about as thick as your thumb. Peel a potato and cut it into strips. Scrape a carrot and cut it into strips.

Wrap the food in doubled foil and place the package on the fire. Cook for fifteen minutes.

A Pocketknife for Campers

If your parents let you own a pocketknife, they know that you know a pocketknife is a tool, not a plaything. A certain kind of pocketknife is useful for campers and hikers. It has a can opener that can cut open such things as cans of beans. It has a bottle opener that can help take off the caps on bottles of pop. It has a blade that can be used for peeling potatoes or scraping carrots—or for whittling.

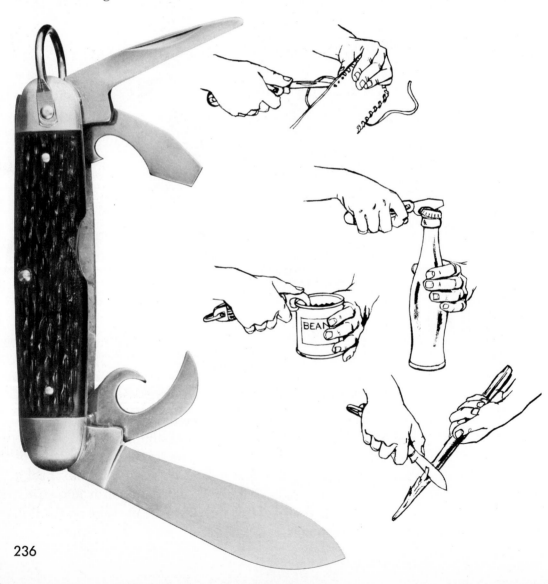

sips, salads, and sandwiches

Hungry? Make a salad, a casserole, a sandwich, or a baked potato. Thirsty? Stir up some lemonade, limeade, orangeade, or hot cocoa. Want something sweet? Bake an instant cake, mix up some date-nut bars, or make an ice-cream cone clown. Those are some of the easy-to-make recipes that you will find on the next pages.

SALADS, SIPS, and SANDWICHES

Before You Begin . . .
MEASURE
CAREFULLY

Measure
large amounts
in a
measuring cup.

Level with a knife.

Measure small amounts with measuring spoons.

REMEMBER

3 teaspoons are the same as 1 tablespoon
4 tablespoons are the same as ¼ cup
16 tablespoons are the same as 1 cup
2 cups are the same as 1 pint
4 cups are the same as 1 quart

LEMONADE

For each glass use

- 2 tablespoons of lemon juice
- 2 tablespoons of sugar
- 1 glass of water

Slice a lemon in half and squeeze the juice into a cup. Take out the seeds.

Pour two tablespoons of juice into a glass. Add sugar.

Add water and stir well.

Taste the lemonade. You may want to add more sugar or more lemon to make it taste just right.

Put in ice cubes.

A drop of red food coloring will make pink lemonade.

LIMEADE and ORANGEADE

To make limeade or orangeade, use a lime or an orange instead of a lemon.

It is even easier to make lemonade or limeade that comes from a can. Empty the frozen lemonade or limeade into a pitcher. Squash it. Then add as much water as the label on the can tells you to.

239

What's for dessert?

MOLDED GELATIN

Use
- 1 package of gelatin dessert
- 1 cup of hot water • 1 cup of cold water
- 1 large mold, or several small molds

Empty a package of gelatin dessert into a large bowl. Break up any lumps with a fork.

Fill a cup with hot water from the faucet and pour it into the bowl. Stir until all the gelatin mix has dissolved.

Then add a cup of cold water. Stir well.

Pour the mixture from the bowl into a large mold or into each of the small ones. Put the mold into the refrigerator.

An hour or two later when the gelatin is firm, take the mold out of the refrigerator. If you dip the mold into a bowl of hot water for just a moment the gelatin will slip out of the mold easily when you turn the mold upside down on a plate.

If you wish, put cream cheese or whipped cream around the gelatin.

ASK FOR HELP

CAKE

It's easy to make a cake from a cake mix that you get at the grocery store.

You add only water to some cake mixes. To others you add only eggs and milk.

Some brands even have a tin-foil cake pan inside the package. And many mixes have a small envelope of powdered frosting hidden inside the flour.

Cake mixes come in many flavors. There are chocolate cakes, yellow cakes, white cakes, orange cakes, lemon cakes, cherry cakes, banana cakes, and spice cakes.

When you make a cake from a mix, always follow the directions on the package carefully. Then you can be sure that your cake will turn out right.

Ask your mother to help you put it in the oven.

ICE-CREAM CONE CLOWNS

For each clown, use
- a dip of ice cream
- an ice-cream cone
- construction paper
- paste, or a stapler
- jelly beans or hard candy for decorations

Cut a strip of construction paper, about two inches wide and eight inches long for the clown collar. Paste or staple the ends together. If you like, cut out a bow tie and paste it to the collar.

Set the collar in a saucer. Place a dip of ice cream on top of it. See Picture.

Stick jelly beans or hard candy on the ice cream for eyes, nose, and mouth.

Place the cone on the ice cream for a hat, and your clown is ready to eat!

241

PUFFY CHEESE SANDWICHES
Use
- slices of bread
- slices of yellow cheese

ASK FOR HELP

SANDWICHES FOR SNACKS OR PARTIES

With a grownup's help, light the oven.

Toast slices of bread in a toaster. When they are brown, remove them with a potholder. Place a slice of cheese on each slice of toast.

Lay the toast on a cookie sheet or aluminum foil and, with a grownup's help, put it on the top rack of the oven.

When the cheese is puffed up and bubbly, a grownup can help you take it out of the oven. When the sandwich has cooled a little, it is ready to eat.

TASTY SANDWICH SPREADS
For two sandwiches use
- $\frac{1}{4}$ cup of canned tuna or potted ham
- 1 hard-boiled egg (boiled egg recipe on page 250 tells how to hard boil an egg)
- 1 tablespoon mayonnaise
- salt

Break the ham or tuna into tiny pieces with a fork. Chop the egg into small pieces. Put the meat and egg together in a bowl. Add mayonnaise and salt.

Mix well.

Spread the mixture over a piece of bread, or toast if you wish. Lay another piece of bread on top, and serve with slices of pickle.

HOT DOGS

Use

- wieners
- hot dog buns
- relish, mustard, or onions

With a grownup's help, fill a saucepan halfway with warm water. Place it over high heat on the stove.

When the water begins to boil, carefully place the wieners into the water so that the hot water won't splash on you. Turn the heat down.

After a few minutes, take the wieners out of the pan with a fork. Let the water drain off.

Place the wieners in the buns.

Add relish, mustard, or onions, if you wish.

Sailboat Salad

Use
- canned peaches
- lettuce
- toothpicks
- paper

Wash a lettuce leaf and lay it on a plate. Place half of a peach on the lettuce, with the round side of the peach down.

Cut a piece of paper so that it looks like a sail. See Picture. Stick a toothpick through the paper to make a mast. Then stick the toothpick into the peach.

If you print the name of each of your guests on the sail, you can use the salads as place cards.

Make a salad just like the sailboat salad, but leave off the sail.

Put cottage cheese or cream cheese in the hollow of the peach. Add a bright, red cherry.

Or fill the peach with mayonnaise, and sprinkle the mayonnaise with chopped nuts.

Tossed Green Salad

ASK FOR HELP

Use
- 1 head of lettuce, chilled
- celery • cucumbers
- onion • tomato
- green peppers
- radish
- carrots
- $\frac{1}{4}$ cup of salad dressing

OIL

Hold a head of lettuce under cold, running water to wash it and loosen the leaves.

Pull the leaves off the head and shake off the water. Break each leaf into about three pieces and place the pieces in a large salad bowl.

Wash the other vegetables for your salad.

Trim leaves off celery, radishes, and carrots.

Now ask a grownup to help you.

Peel carrots, onion, and cucumbers.

Cut cores out of peppers.

Cut the vegetables into thin slices, or small pieces. Put everything into the salad bowl with the lettuce.

245

Just before you put the salad on the table, pour your salad dressing over it. Then with a large fork and spoon, mix or "toss" the vegetables to cover them with dressing.

a meal in one dish

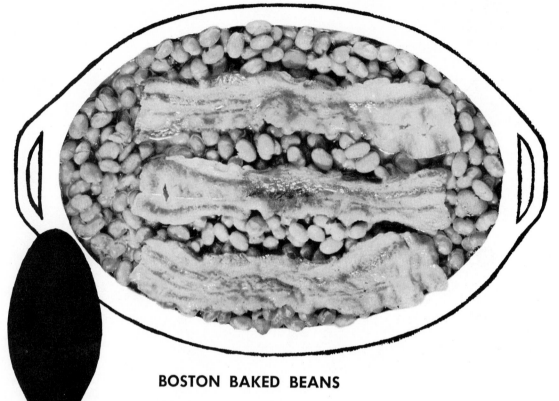

BOSTON BAKED BEANS

Use

- 1 can of baked beans
- 1 tablespoon of catsup
- 1 tablespoon of molasses, or sirup
- 4 or 5 slices of bacon • 1 onion

With a grownup's help, light the oven and set it at 350 degrees.

Open a can of beans and pour them into a heavy baking dish.

Slice an onion and separate it into rings.

Add onion rings, molasses, and catsup to the beans. Mix well.

Cut bacon slices in half and arrange them on top of the beans.

With help, set the baking dish into the oven. Take it out in about 45 minutes.

ASK FOR HELP

ASK FOR HELP

TUNA DELIGHT

Use

- 1 can of tuna fish
- 1 can of mushroom soup
- ¼ cup of milk
- potato chips (about ½ of a medium-sized package)

With a grownup's help, light the oven and set it at 325 degrees.

Put some potato chips into a bowl. Break them into small pieces by pressing them against the bowl.

Empty a can of tuna fish into another bowl. Break up the pieces.

Put the potato chips into the bowl with the tuna fish. Add a can of mushroom soup and ¼ cup of milk. Mix everything together.

Rub a pat of butter or margarine around the inside of a baking dish.

Pour the tuna fish mixture into the baking dish.

With help, set the dish into the hot oven and take it out in an hour.

ASK FOR HELP

BAKED POTATOES

Use

- large potatoes (Idaho potatoes are good)
- butter or margarine
- salt and pepper

The oven should be lighted and set at 375 degrees.

Wash the potatoes clean with cold water and a vegetable brush.

With a grownup's help, put the potatoes on the rack in the center of the oven. Be careful not to touch the rack.

Let the potatoes bake for about one hour, or until they are soft enough to stick a fork into easily. With help, take the potatoes out of the oven, using a potholder or a long-handled fork.

Cut an "X" with a knife on top of the potatoes.

Squeeze each potato to burst it open. The potatoes will be hot, so you may need help with this. Put salt, pepper, and butter in the opening.

OUTDOOR BAKED POTATOES

Instead of putting the scrubbed potatoes in the oven, wrap them in aluminum foil.

Put the wrapped potatoes in the hot coals of an outdoor fire. Your father or mother can help you do this. Rake hot coals on top of them.

Let the potatoes bake 30 minutes if they are small, or as much as 45 minutes if they are large.

Unwrap the potatoes. They will be hot, so hold the potato with a potholder and pull away the foil with a fork.

WITH POTATOES

POTATO SALAD

Use

- potatoes • celery
- salt and pepper • 2 eggs
- mayonnaise • 1 onion
- large lettuce leaves

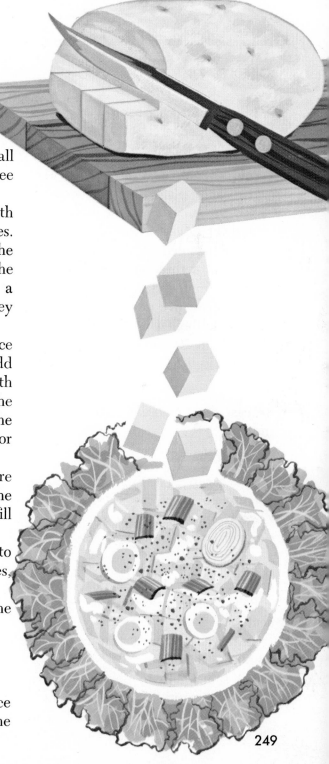

Peel potatoes and cut them into small cubes. Cut enough cubes to fill three cups.

Place the cubes in a saucepan, with enough water to cover all the pieces. Add one-half teaspoon of salt. Cover the saucepan and with help place it on the stove to cook. When you can stick a fork through the potatoes easily, they are ready to take off the stove.

While the potatoes are cooking, place two eggs into another saucepan. Add enough water to cover them. With help, heat them on the stove until the water reaches a boil. Then turn the fire low and leave the eggs on it for 20 more minutes.

While the potatoes and eggs are cooking, chop the onion. Also cut the celery into small pieces, enough to fill one cup.

Peel the eggs and chop them into small pieces. Mix the eggs, potatoes, celery, and onion together.

Add enough mayonnaise to make the pieces stick to each other.

Add a pinch of salt and pepper.

Mix well.

Keep the salad in the refrigerator.

When it's mealtime, arrange lettuce leaves in a salad bowl, and put the salad on top of them.

Breakfast

BOILED EGGS

Use
- 2 eggs for each person
- salt and pepper

SOFT

Wash the eggs and put them into a saucepan.

Pour in enough water to cover the eggs.

With help, place the pan over a medium flame until the water begins to boil. Lower the heat a little until tiny bubbles form around the edges of the pan.

MEDIUM

For soft-boiled eggs, take the eggs out of the water with a spoon two or three minutes after you lower the heat.

For medium-soft eggs, take the eggs out of the water with a spoon four or five minutes after you lower the heat.

For hard-boiled eggs, take the eggs out of the water with a spoon about 20 minutes after you lower the heat.

HARD

Run cold water over the eggs, and get help to take off shells.

TOAST

Toast slices of bread in a toaster. Spread the toast with butter and jam.

HOT COCOA

For each cup
- 1 tablespoon of cocoa
- 1 tablespoon of sugar
- 2 tablespoons of water
- 1 cup of milk
- a marshmallow, or cinnamon, if you wish

To make one cup of cocoa, put the cocoa, sugar, and water into a cup. Stir until it is mixed together.

Pour milk into a saucepan, and with help, place it over low heat.

Heat the milk until tiny bubbles form around the edges, but do not let it boil.

Get some help to pour the hot milk into the cup with the cocoa mixture in it. Stir until all of the cocoa is mixed in.

To make a foamy drink, drop a marshmallow into the cocoa. Or sprinkle cinnamon on top to give it a special taste.

FAST and SIMPLE

It's easy to cook a delicious breakfast for yourself
or for the whole family.

ASK FOR
HELP

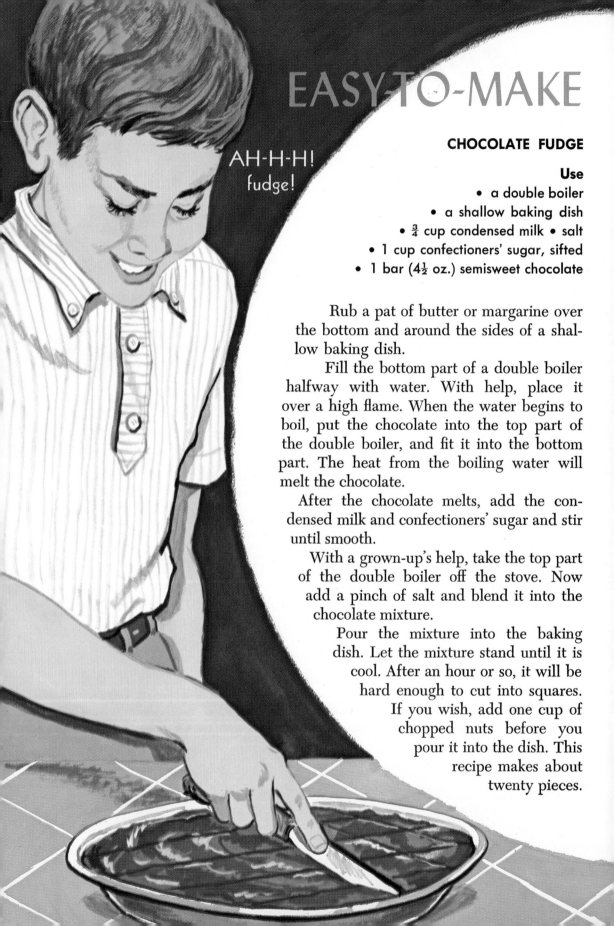

EASY-TO-MAKE

AH-H-H!
fudge!

CHOCOLATE FUDGE

Use
- a double boiler
- a shallow baking dish
- $\frac{3}{4}$ cup condensed milk • salt
- 1 cup confectioners' sugar, sifted
- 1 bar ($4\frac{1}{2}$ oz.) semisweet chocolate

Rub a pat of butter or margarine over the bottom and around the sides of a shallow baking dish.

Fill the bottom part of a double boiler halfway with water. With help, place it over a high flame. When the water begins to boil, put the chocolate into the top part of the double boiler, and fit it into the bottom part. The heat from the boiling water will melt the chocolate.

After the chocolate melts, add the condensed milk and confectioners' sugar and stir until smooth.

With a grown-up's help, take the top part of the double boiler off the stove. Now add a pinch of salt and blend it into the chocolate mixture.

Pour the mixture into the baking dish. Let the mixture stand until it is cool. After an hour or so, it will be hard enough to cut into squares. If you wish, add one cup of chopped nuts before you pour it into the dish. This recipe makes about twenty pieces.

CANDIES

UNCOOKED FONDANT

Use

- 1 egg white   • a damp cloth
- 1 teaspoon vanilla
- 1 tablespoon cold water
- sifted confectioners' sugar
- 2 tablespoons condensed milk

I'm
very fond
of fondant

Ask your mother to show you how to separate the yolk from the white of the egg. Pour the yolk into a small bowl and put it into the refrigerator. Pour the white into a large mixing bowl. The egg white is all you use to make this kind of candy.

Add water, milk, and vanilla to egg white. Beat with a fork until they are well mixed.

Sift the confectioners' sugar with a flour sifter. Slowly pour the sugar into the mixture and stir well. Keep adding sugar until the mixture is thick and stiff enough to pick up gobs of it. Be sure your hands are clean. Squeeze the mixture with your fingers until it is smooth.

Cover the bowl with a damp cloth.

After about an hour, take the cloth off. With clean hands, pick up lumps of the mixture and shape them into small balls. Roll each ball in confectioners' sugar, and your candy is ready to eat.

If you wish, stick a cherry, a walnut, or raisins in the center of the ball to make it look pretty.

ASK FOR HELP

253

Make A Dessert Without Cooking

Sometimes it's fun to mix flour and water
into dough, roll it out with a rolling pin,
and cut it into different shapes.
But that's just for playing—not for eating.
If you want a mixture that you can eat,
and don't have to cook,
try this recipe.

DATE-NUT BARS

Use
- 1½ cups of graham cracker crumbs
- ¼ teaspoon of salt
- 1 cup of chopped dates
- 1 cup of chopped nuts
- 1 cup of small marshmallow pieces
- 1 cup of heavy cream

With a rolling pin, crush graham crackers
into fine crumbs until you have 1½ cups.
In a bowl, mix the graham cracker crumbs,
salt, chopped dates, chopped nuts, and
marshmallow pieces.

Then, pour in the heavy cream
a little at a time, and stir
until the graham cracker crumbs are moist.

Finally, spoon the mixture out of the bowl
into a medium-sized cake pan.
Spread the mixture evenly in the pan
and refrigerate.

When chilled, slice into small square bars.

popcorn

Use
- popcorn (¾ cup will make 2 quarts)
- vegetable oil, or margarine • salt
- popcorn popper, or deep pan with lid

Pour in enough vegetable oil to cover the bottom of the popper.

With a grownup's help, place the popcorn popper over a high heat.

When the oil is hot, pour in the popcorn. Cover with a lid.

As soon as the popcorn begins to pop, turn the heat down as low as it will go.

Shake the pan often to keep the corn from burning.

When the popcorn stops popping, pour it into a large bowl. Add salt.

POPCORN BALLS

To make 6 large popcorn balls, use
- 2 quarts popcorn, already popped
- 1 cup molasses • ½ cup corn sirup
- 1½ tablespoons of butter or margarine

Pour the molasses and corn sirup into a saucepan and stir them together.

Place the pan over a high flame. With a grownup's help, stir the sirup until it comes to a boil.

Drip some sirup from a spoon into a cup of cold water. When the sirup forms a hard ball in the water, the sirup is ready to take off the flame.

Mix butter or margarine into the sirup. Pour the sirup over the popcorn. Before you begin, rub butter over your hands so that the popcorn balls will not stick to you. When the sirup-covered popcorn is cool enough to hold, press it into popcorn balls.

256

Are you going on a trip to the zoo, to the airport, to the beach, to a museum, or are you just going on a walk around town? Here are some ideas that will make your next trip lots of fun.

trips and visits

FUN

Much of the fun of any trip or visit is the ride in a car, a bus, or a train. As you whiz by, you can see large cities, small towns, green farms, billboards, animals, trees, cars, and trucks from the window.

Here are some games to play as you ride.

License-Plate Games

Each rider writes down the numbers 0, 1, 2, 3, 4, 5, 6, 7, 8, and 9 on a sheet of paper. When he sees a car with a license plate beginning with one of these numbers, he marks a line through the number on his paper.

The first person to mark off all his numbers is the winner.

Another license-plate game is played by spotting license plates from as many states as you can. Write down the name of each state you see on a license plate. The person with the most states is the winner.

ON THE WAY

Alphabet Fun

For this game the riders must find all the letters of the alphabet on billboards along the road. First, find a word on a billboard beginning with "A." Then find a word on the next billboard beginning with "B." Watch the billboards until you have found words beginning with all the letters of the alphabet.

Sing a Song

As you ride along, have someone start to sing. Everyone joins in. At the first crossroad, another person starts a different song, and everyone joins in. At the next crossroad, a third person starts another song. Keep changing songs at every crossroad for as long as you want the game to last.

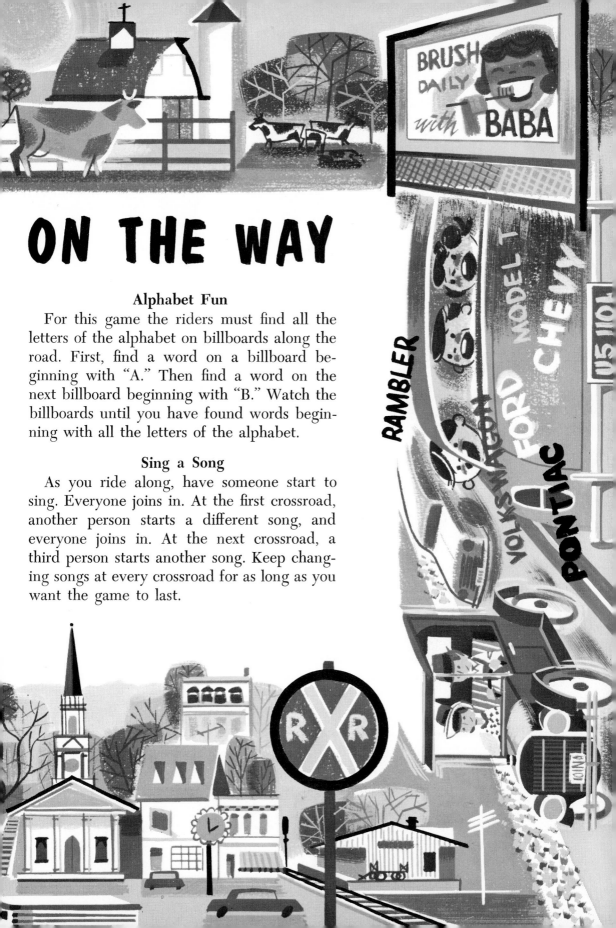

TRAVEL

ADD-A-MOTION

Someone begins the game by making motions. The person may wiggle his thumbs. The second person wiggles his thumbs and adds a new motion, such as pulling his ears. The next person wiggles his thumbs, pulls his ears, and adds a new motion, such as clapping his hands.

The game continues, with each person doing all the motions and adding a new one. The person who can do the most motions without getting mixed up is the winner.

HIDE AND SEEK

Pretend you are a tiny speck and that you are hiding in the car. The other riders ask questions like, "Are you inside the car? Are you on the hood? Are you under the seat?" You answer "yes" or "no."

The person who guesses your hiding place can be the next one to pretend to hide.

GAMES

WHAT ANIMAL AM I?

The person who starts the game decides what animal he wants to be. The other riders try to guess what he is. They take turns asking questions like, "Can you fly? Are you red? Do you live in water?" You answer "yes" or "no."

The one who guesses what animal the person is gets to be the next animal.

MY FATHER OWNS A STORE

Choose someone to be IT. IT says, "My father owns a grocery store, and he sells something beginning with a 'B.'" He may be thinking of butter or bread.

Each of the players gets one guess. If they do not guess the right answer, IT starts over again. He says, "My father owns a grocery store and he sells something beginning with a 'C.'" He may be thinking of carrots. Everyone gets another guess.

The person who guesses the right answer is the new IT.

VISIT

A

MUSEUM

There are many different kinds of museums to visit.

HISTORY MUSEUM—collections of things belonging to people of other times and other lands

NATURAL HISTORY MUSEUM—stuffed animals and bones of animals that show the history of the animals that have lived on the earth

ART MUSEUM—paintings, statues, and art crafts made by ancient and modern artists

SCIENCE MUSEUM—exhibits showing the parts of things and how things work—tools, machines, radios, rocks, trees, and scientific instruments

HEALTH MUSEUM—exhibits and diagrams of the parts of the body and how to take care of them

PLANETARIUM—displays of telescopes, and pictures and models of the planets, moon, and stars, as well as a moving picture overhead of all the stars in the sky

AQUARIUM—tanks of fresh and salt-water fish, turtles, and other sea life

TRAILSIDE MUSEUM—exhibits of animals, plants, flowers, and rocks that can be found near the museum

PLAN AHEAD

Find out the hours the museum will be open. Ask how much it will cost to get in.

Most large museums have special tours with guides to explain the interesting things in each room. If you plan to take one of these trips, find out the time it will begin. Museums have guards who will be glad to answer your questions.

Most museums have so many things to see that you cannot see all of them in one visit. It is best to plan to see only part of the museum at a time.

Take along a notebook and a pencil to write down the interesting things you see, or draw sketches to show your friends.

After your visit, you can get books at a library telling about the things you found most interesting at the museum.

263

A TRIP TO

FEED the SEALS
FRESH FISH
FOR ONLY 5¢

FISH

A trip to the zoo is exciting. There are all sorts of wild animals living in cages or in fenced areas made to look like their homes in faraway lands. At most zoos there are special houses for different kinds of animals.

LION HOUSE—lions, tigers, panthers, wildcats, leopards, and jaguars

MONKEY HOUSE—monkeys, chimpanzees, apes, and gorillas

ELEPHANT HOUSE—African and Indian elephants

REPTILE HOUSE—snakes, lizards, turtles, crocodiles, and alligators

BIRD HOUSE—parrots, parakeets, and other birds

Animals such as bears, wolves, giraffes, deer, and zebras live outdoors behind fences.

CHILDREN'S ZOO—a zoo where all the animals can be handled by children

THE ZOO

PLAN AHEAD

The best time to visit the zoo is around feeding time. Then you can see what kinds of food the animals eat and how they eat it. Ask your mother to call or write to the zoo to find out the feeding times.

Always follow the rules at the zoo. The rules are made to keep the animals healthy and happy so you can enjoy them. At some zoos you can feed peanuts to the animals.

There may be signs on or near the animal cages that give the name of the animal, where the animal usually lives, and how old the animal is. If you cannot read the signs, ask a grownup to read them to you.

After your visit, begin a zoo scrapbook by cutting out magazine pictures of the animals you saw at the zoo.

A DAY AT THE BEACH

The beach makes a wonderful playground for all kinds of games in the sand and the water. Here are some ways to have fun at the beach.

SAND BUILDING

You can build sand castles, tunnels, dams, lakes, tiny cities, even people and animals out of sand.

The sand near the water is damp and hard. Dig up the hard sand and pile it into the shape you want.

SHELLS and PEBBLES

Most beaches are covered with little shells and tiny pebbles.

See how many different shells and pebbles you can find. Start a collection with the ones you find at the beach and add to it when you find more.

SPOKE TAG

Pick a place on the beach that has hard, damp sand. Run around in a circle to make the shape of a wheel with your footprints. Then run across the circle to make footprints for spokes.

Play a game of tag on the wheel and spoke lines. Everyone must run only on the lines. The person who is IT must tag another person without reaching across or running across the lines.

WATER TAG

Be sure a grownup is near when you play this game.

Before you can play, learn to blow bubbles in the water.

Put your face in the water and blow air through your nose to make bubbles. When you have blown out all the air, lift your head out of the water and take a deep breath.

No one can be tagged if his face is in the water. When the players see IT coming toward them, they duck their faces in the water and blow bubbles until he passes by.

267

You don't have to travel to faraway places to see and do interesting things. A visit around your own town can be exciting and fun.

CONSTRUCTION WORK

Everyone likes to watch a building going up—whether it is a house, a school, or a tall skyscraper.

If one is being built nearby, you can visit it many times to see how it grows. You might want to keep a notebook on what part is built each day. You can write down the date the bulldozers dig the basement, the date the first wall is laid, and the date the windows and doors are added. Or you can make a model of the new building with blocks of wood, adding another block each time the building goes one story higher.

THE CITY PARK

There are lots of things to do at the city park. You can swing, slide, run, and play in the playground. Some parks have ponds where you can fish or sail your boat.

Some parks have outdoor tables for picnics, and sometimes even stoves where you can roast wieners or marshmallows.

YOUR TOWN

DEPARTMENT STORE

Department stores sell lots of things. It's fun to visit a department store and see all the interesting displays of goods.

Most department stores have elevators or escalators to carry customers from one floor to another. When you ride an escalator, you can look down at the people in the store. They look very small from where you're standing.

After you have seen what a big store is like, you might want to play "store" at home. Use a large paper carton for an elevator or for a display counter.

THE FIRE STATION

The firemen at the fire station will be glad to show you around the fire station. You will see shiny red fire engines and the firemen's big rubber boots, coats, and helmets. In most fire stations there is a long pole for the firemen to slide down when they hear the alarm.

While you are at the fire station, perhaps you can sit behind the wheel of the fire engine and wear a fireman's helmet.

After your visit, draw pictures of the fire engines and the firemen's clothes. If you have a toy fire engine, you can pretend you're hurrying to a big fire.

269

DOTS AND LINES

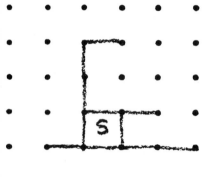

All you need for this game is a sheet of paper and a pencil for each player. Someone makes a square with many dots on the paper. See Picture. Then the players take turns drawing a line between any two dots in the square.

A player can connect only two dots at a time. He may draw a line up and down, or straight across. If the line he draws closes up a small box in the square, he gets to draw another line, and he puts his initial in the box.

The game is over when all the lines have been drawn. The player who has the most boxes with his initial in them is the winner.

PICTURE JOKES

To make picture jokes, you will need a sheet of paper and a pencil for each player.

Each player folds his paper in three parts, as shown. Then he draws the head of an animal or a person on the top fold, making sure that the neck is drawn down over the second fold. Each person folds his paper so no one can see what he has drawn and then passes it to another player. The second player draws the body of an animal or a person. He draws legs across the fold of the next section of the paper. Then he folds the paper so no one can see the body he has drawn, and hands it to another player. The last player draws the legs and feet of an animal or a person.

When the drawing is finished, unfold the paper and you will see a funny picture joke.

WAITING CAN BE FUN

On some trips and visits you must spend time waiting for a bus, or a train, or car repairs.

Here are some games to play while you wait.

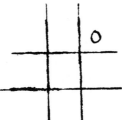

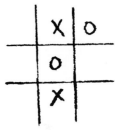

TICKTACKTOE

Here's a game for two players only.

Draw four lines on a sheet of paper. Two lines should cross the other two. One of the players begins the game by making an X in one of the spaces. The other player makes an O in another space. The one who gets three X's or three O's in a straight line—up, diagonally, or sideways—is the winner.

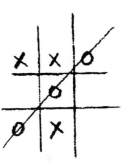

A VISIT TO THE AIRPORT

CONTROL TOWER — RUNWAY — TERMINAL BUILDING — OBSERVATION DECK — TAXIWAY — LIGHTS

There are many things to see at an airport. See if you can find:

AIRPLANES—airplanes of all sizes landing and taking off every few minutes

RUNWAYS—long concrete or asphalt paths where airplanes land and take off

TAXIWAYS—short concrete paths that airplanes follow when they move from one place to another on the ground

HANGARS—large buildings where airplanes are kept when they are not flying

LIGHTS—colored lights to signal the pilots where to land and take off

TERMINAL BUILDING—where passengers buy tickets, check luggage, and wait for planes to come in

OBSERVATION DECK—usually on top of the terminal building, where visitors can watch planes land and take off

CONTROL TOWER—tower on top of the terminal building, where operators radio the pilot weather conditions and when and where to land

LOUDSPEAKER—a device for announcing arrivals and departures of airplanes.

After your visit, you can make a model airport out of cardboard boxes and clay.

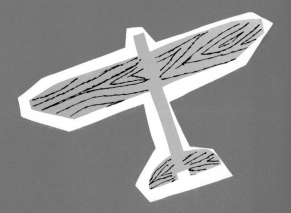

collecting and other hobbies

What do you collect—stamps or stones, coins or cards, shells or soldiers? Or is your hobby building things—like model boats or model planes? Or are pets your hobby—your dog, your cat, your parakeet? Or are you looking for a new hobby? See the next pages.

COLLECTING TOYS

PAPER DOLLS

There are many kinds of paper dolls to collect.

Paper dolls can be bought at a dime store. They do not cost very much. Or you can make your own paper dolls by cutting out pictures from magazines and newspapers.

TOY SOLDIERS

You can collect a whole army of toy soldiers made of tin, wood, or plastic. Some may be dressed in fancy uniforms, and some may be sitting on prancing horses. Others may be ready for battle, carrying guns and shoulder packs. You can have soldiers from other countries. Or start a collection of only Civil War soldiers or only modern soldiers.

MARBLES

There are many sizes and colors of marbles to collect. Perhaps you will want a collection of only one color, or collections of agates and shooters only.

You can display your marbles in a box with corrugated paper in the bottom. The ridges in the paper keep the marbles from rolling all around in the box.

There are many other kinds of toys you can collect such as stuffed animals, beads, model airplanes and ships, doll dishes, records, and masks.

MINIATURES

Miniatures are tiny copies of large things. There are tiny tea-cups, dolls, cars, boats, airplanes, furniture, fans, books, and animals. Perhaps you can start your own collection with the miniatures you find in cereal boxes and in gum machines.

You can mount miniatures by running a string through them, or by crossing a string over them, and tying the string to a piece of cardboard. Or you can put miniatures on a bookshelf.

Collecting Things Made of Paper

MATCHBOOK COVERS

You can find fancy matchbooks in restaurants, hotels, and drugstores, and they are usually given away. Perhaps you will want to collect only matchbooks with pictures of birds, or only matchbooks of one color or one design.

You can paste your collection in a scrapbook. Or make your own display cards. Get a large piece of cardboard and fasten two or three long strings or cords across it. See Picture. Hang the matchbook covers over the string.

Make sure that there are no matches left in the book before you add them to your collection.

PLAYING CARDS

Collecting playing cards is a popular hobby. You can trade with other persons who collect cards.

The pictures on the backs of cards may be of famous paintings, birds, flowers, landscapes, or fancy designs. Perhaps you can find miniature cards, too.

You can keep your card collection in a box decorated with some of your cards. Or you can use your collection to decorate a wastebasket or a tray.

MENUS AND PROGRAMS

Collecting menus and programs from places you have visited is an easy way to remember good times. Paste your collection in a large scrapbook. Or you may have two scrapbooks—one for the places you have visited and another for places your friends have visited.

PICTURE POSTCARDS

Picture postcards are easy to collect. Almost every city or town has postcards showing its buildings, parks, rivers, or outdoor scenes. You can begin your collection with the postcards that come to your home. Ask your friends to save their cards for you, too.

You may want to collect postcards from only one country, state, or city. Or you may collect only postcards with pictures of fountains or tall buildings.

You can display your collection of cards on sheets of cardboard or on a bulletin board in your room. Arrange the cards according to the pictures on them, or arrange the cards in a fancy design on the cardboard.

STAMPS

Stamp collecting is a popular hobby. You can begin a stamp collection with any unusual stamps you find around home. Ask your friends to save stamps for you, too.

Also, you can buy packets of different kinds of stamps at a hobby store or a stationery store. If you get two stamps that are alike, trade your extra stamp with another stamp collector.

The best place to keep your stamps is in a stamp album. Mount the stamps with paper hinges. You can arrange them in the album according to country, color, size, or design.

AND COINS

COINS

Coin collecting is much like stamp collecting. It is best to start your collection with small coins such as pennies, nickels, and dimes. If you have a Canadian penny, you may want to start a collection of Canadian coins. Or you can start a copper collection with copper coins from all over the world. Also, you might try to get one coin, such as a penny, nickel, or dime, for as many years back as you can. Maybe you could get Lincoln pennies from 1909 to now.

Make display sheets out of heavy cardboard with holes cut in it to fit each coin. Mount the coins according to size, type, or year.

Other favorite collections are souvenirs, travel folders, tags and labels, flags and banners, campaign items, emblems, and salt and pepper shakers.

COLLECTING THINGS OF BEAUTY

CORDS, BRAIDS, AND RIBBONS

Cords, braids, and ribbons come in all kinds of beautiful soft materials. There are satins, velvets, rayons, and silks—all in pretty colors. Try to find many different kinds of colors of materials for your collection.

You can display the collection on sheets of cardboard. Make a picture with your collection by framing the cardboard with heavy braid or cord. Then arrange the pieces of ribbon in a fancy design and pin them to the cardboard.

LACES AND CLOTHS

Tiny pieces of lace and cloth left over from sewing are nice to collect.

Paste your collection on sheets of cardboard or in a scrapbook. Cover the page or sheet with cellophane to keep the collection fresh and clean. You can arrange the items in your collection according to size, material, or color. Or you can display your lace collection on a piece of velvet or dark cloth.

You can also use your collection to make pictures that you can feel, called "collages." A collage can be used for a scrapbook cover or as a picture for the wall.

BUTTONS AND BUCKLES

You can start a collection with the buttons and buckles you find around your home. Buttons and buckles may be round, square, or oblong, gold, silver, or colored, large, small, plain, or fancy. You may want to collect only one kind of button or buckle, for example, only square-shaped buttons or buckles.

You can make a display of your collection by putting the buttons and buckles into little matchboxes that have been glued in shoebox lids. As your collection grows, you can mount it on sheets of cardboard. Put all the buttons of one color or shape on a separate sheet.

BEAUTIFUL BOTTLES

Many things your mother buys come in bottles. When the bottles are empty, use the most interesting ones for a bottle collection. Be sure to wash out the bottles and scrape off the labels. You can paint designs on the bottles or glue tiny seashells or beads on them.

Arrange your collection on a shelf or a window sill so everyone can see them.

Other beautiful things you can collect are old jewelry, hat feathers and plumes, figurines, plates and pitchers, glassware, and hand-painted fans.

LEAVES

There are many kinds of leaves. You may want to collect only one kind at a time. Start by collecting broad leaves, or narrow leaves, or autumn leaves. Some people collect green leaves in the summer, and hunt for the same kinds of leaves in the fall when they have changed colors.

When you gather leaves, take only the ones with stems attached. Your leaves will keep their color for a long time if you place each leaf on a newspaper, cover it with a sheet of wax paper, and press it with a hot iron.

Or press the leaf between the pages of a big book. When the leaf becomes flat and crisp, paste it in a leaf scrapbook.

NATURE

FERNS

If you live near cool, damp woods, you can start a collection of ferns. Some fern leaves are shaped like hearts, and others are long and narrow.

Ferns should be placed on a newspaper, covered with wax paper, and pressed with a hot iron before they are pasted in a fern scrapbook. Ferns will stay pretty a long time if you cover each page with a sheet of cellophane paper.

WILD FLOWERS

Place each flower between two sheets of newspaper before putting it into a big book. The newspaper will soak up the water from the flower so it won't become moldy. Change the paper several times until the flower is flat and dry. Then tape the flower in your flower scrapbook and cover it with cellophane.

Other things you can collect from the woods or fields are seeds, acorns, bark from trees, and even birds' nests.

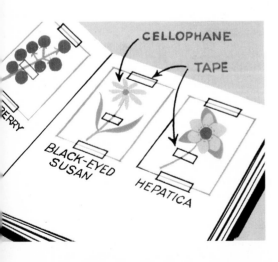

ASPEN

COLLECTIONS

SUGAR
MAPLE

ACORNS

MAPLE
SEEDS

LICORICE FERN

SILVERY
SPLEENWORT

RED CLOVER

VIOLET

WILD
ROSE

SUNFLOWER

283

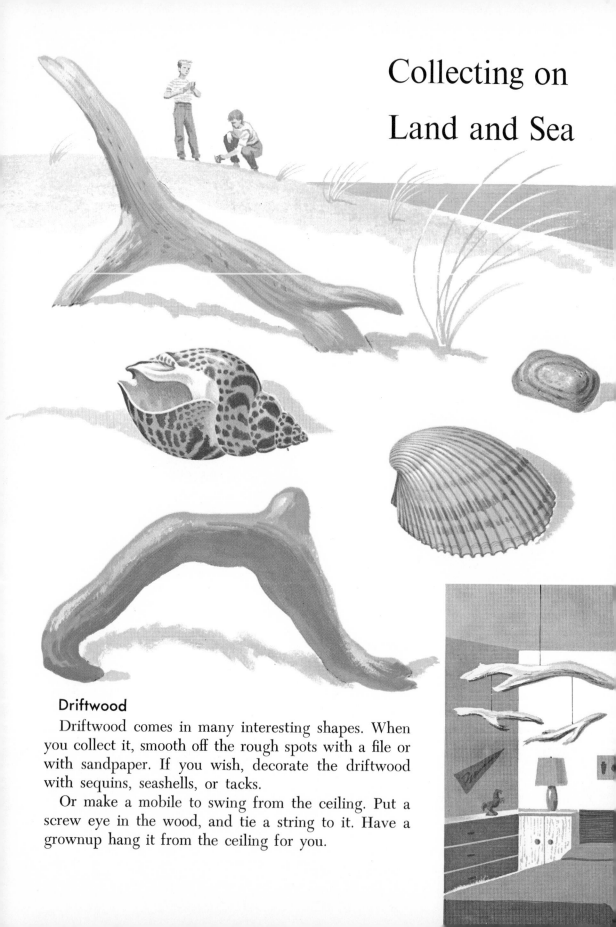

Collecting on Land and Sea

Driftwood

Driftwood comes in many interesting shapes. When you collect it, smooth off the rough spots with a file or with sandpaper. If you wish, decorate the driftwood with sequins, seashells, or tacks.

Or make a mobile to swing from the ceiling. Put a screw eye in the wood, and tie a string to it. Have a grownup hang it from the ceiling for you.

Shells

You can find shells of all shapes, sizes, and colors on the beach or near a river. Some are fan-shaped, some are spiral-shaped, and others are shaped like trumpets. They may be gray, pink, or even purple.

Mount the shells on sheets of cardboard with tape or glue. Put sizes, shapes, colors, or kinds of shells together. Or make things out of your shells. Shells with holes in them can be strung for bracelets and necklaces. Large clamshells can be used for ash trays. Tiny shells can be glued to little boxes or to earring and pin frames, which you can buy at a dime store.

Rocks and Stones

Rocks and stones are easy to find. Look for different kinds—flat, round, smooth, rough, and bright-colored ones. Don't pass up a rock or stone because it is covered with dirt. When it is washed and polished, it may be pretty.

Also, stones that look plain on the outside may be beautiful on the inside. Crack some of the stones in half with a hammer to see how they look on the inside.

Plain stones may look beautiful when they are in water. You can display these stones in a glass or jar of water.

Some people collect butterflies, moths, snail shells, Indian arrowheads, and samples of wood.

285

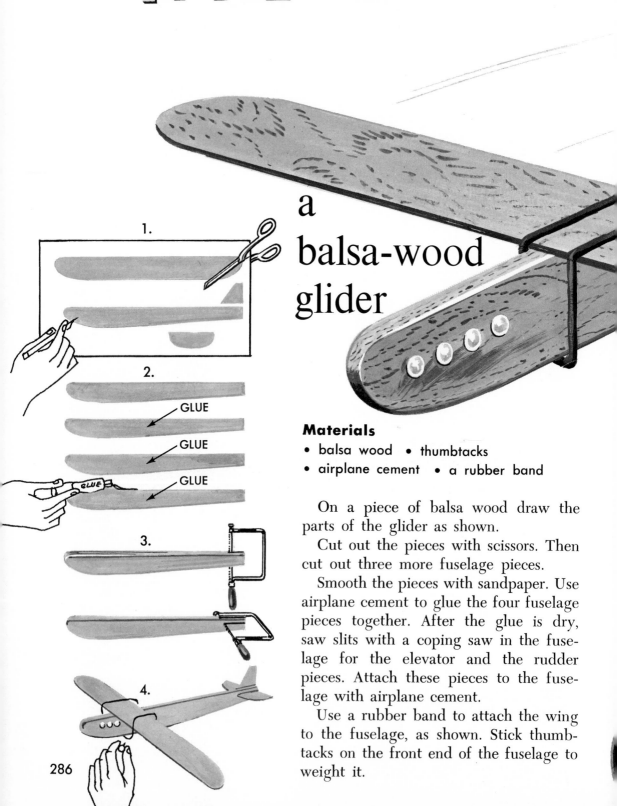

1.

2.

GLUE

GLUE

GLUE

3.

4.

a balsa-wood glider

Materials
- balsa wood
- thumbtacks
- airplane cement
- a rubber band

On a piece of balsa wood draw the parts of the glider as shown.

Cut out the pieces with scissors. Then cut out three more fuselage pieces.

Smooth the pieces with sandpaper. Use airplane cement to glue the four fuselage pieces together. After the glue is dry, saw slits with a coping saw in the fuselage for the elevator and the rudder pieces. Attach these pieces to the fuselage with airplane cement.

Use a rubber band to attach the wing to the fuselage, as shown. Stick thumbtacks on the front end of the fuselage to weight it.

286

WOOD

model kits

It's easy to make model airplanes, cars, and boats from model kits. You can buy the kits at hobby stores, department stores, drugstores, and dime stores. The kits do not cost very much, and they usually include everything you need to build the model. But always check to see if they have a model knife, glue, sandpaper, and paint. If these are not in the kit, you will have to buy them.

model

building

with

plastic

You can build model ships, airplanes, old and new cars, rockets, trains, guns, animals, and even human skeletons with put-together plastic kits.

The parts in the kits are already shaped. Just fit them together and glue them in place. When finished, the model usually looks like the real thing.

You can buy plastic model kits at a dime store, hobby shop, or even at some supermarkets and drugstores. Some kits are harder to make than others. The less expensive ones have fewer parts and are usually easier to make.

There are directions in every kit. Follow them closely, step by step. Often each piece has a number printed in the plastic so that it is easy to find it on the directions.

Glue only one piece at a time. Be sure to cover your worktable with newspapers. This way the glue will not get on the furniture.

Use only the special plastic glue that comes in tubes. Put a hole in the end of the tube with a straight pin. Then the hole will be small enough so that the glue comes out only a little at a time.

Be sure to set each part aside if the directions say to let it dry before gluing another part to it. Otherwise you may bend it out of shape, and it will dry in the wrong position.

Raising Pets

Before you choose a pet, find out what the pet eats, how much room it needs to play, and whether it should live indoors or outdoors.

dogs and puppies

When you get a dog for a pet, you must feed it and take care of it.

FOOD—Puppies should be fed lots of milk, cereal, and crumbled bread, three or four times a day. Older dogs need canned dog food, cereal, and milk, once or twice a day. Always keep fresh water in a pan near the place where you feed your dog.

SHELTER—If your dog lives indoors, make him a bed by putting shredded paper or a blanket in a cardboard box. Dogs that live outdoors need a doghouse.

TRAINING—Start teaching your puppy tricks while he is young. Teach him only one trick at a time and have him do it over and over. When he does the trick correctly, reward him with a puppy treat.

cats and kittens

Taking care of cats is easy. They wash themselves every day and eat almost any food.

FOOD—Cats like to drink milk and cream, but they need to be fed fish, beef, liver, and other kinds of meat.

SHELTER—Cats need a clean, dry bed at night. You can use a basket or a cardboard box for your cat's bed.

TRAINING—Cats like to play with a rubber ball or chase a string. They also like to hook their claws into sofas and chairs. You can make a scratching post for your cat by wrapping an old piece of carpeting around a soft piece of wood. Sprinkle the scratching post with mint or catnip, which cats like to smell.

hamsters

Hamsters make interesting pets, but they need more care than dogs or cats.

FOOD—Hamsters like different things to eat, such as carrots, lettuce, celery, bread, dog biscuit, grain, or guinea pig food. They need fresh water every day.

SHELTER—Hamsters need metal cages because they can chew through wood. The bottom of the cage should be filled with cedar chips, sawdust, wood shavings, or excelsior for the hamster's nest and hiding place for food. The cages should be scrubbed every week.

Hamsters bite when they are frightened, so be careful when you handle them. It is best to wear gloves.

PETS

in Bowls and Cages

Goldfish

Before you buy goldfish, you should make a home for them. A tank or a bowl like the ones shown here is best. Get some sand and wash it by running water over it. Then pour the sand into the bowl and plant some water plants at the back and sides of the bowl or tank. These plants give off oxygen for the fish. Fill the bowl with water.

Do not crowd the tank with too many fish. A medium-sized bowl or tank should not have more than two fish in it.

Fish need to be fed only a few times a week. Give them only as much food as they can eat in 10 minutes. Goldfish like to eat worms and flies, in addition to the prepared fish food that you can buy at pet stores.

Turtles and Frogs

Pet turtles and frogs need a home with both land and water. Pour clean sand about two fingers deep into a fish tank. Push the sand up into a hill at one end of the tank. Put some plants in the sand to shade the pets. Then pile pebbles, rocks, and soil on the slope. See Picture. Put enough fresh water into the tank to fill one end, leaving the sand hill dry.

If you wish, you can use dirt instead of sand. But you will have to put the water in a large dish at one end of the tank.

Place wire screening over the top of the tank to keep the pets from climbing out.

Parakeets and Canaries

Before you get a bird, you should get a cage for it. Hang the cage away from drafts because birds catch colds easily. Put a thick newspaper in the bottom of the cage and sprinkle it with fine gravel. Give your pet fresh water and birdseed every day. Birds also like celery and lettuce.

Some parakeets can be taught to say a few words. Start teaching the bird to talk while it is young. Say the words over and over, and the bird will soon learn to repeat them.

Canaries are popular pets because of their beautiful song. Canaries sing more often if you have two of them and keep them in separate cages. Then the two canaries may sing to each other.

INDOOR GARDENS

You can grow a garden in your own room and have fun watching it grow.

A WATER GARDEN

Vegetables can make a pretty water garden. Carrots and horseradishes grow well in water. Sweet potatoes grow long, trailing vines.

Lay a large sweet potato in a shallow dish and pour in enough water to half-cover it. Cut a few inches from the tops of carrots and horseradishes and set them in the water. See Picture.

Set your garden in or near a large window. Check the water every few days to make sure that there is enough.

A HOTHOUSE GARDEN

Grow a tiny hothouse garden in a fish tank, or glass jar. Use glass for a cover.

Put a layer of charcoal in the bottom of the bowl or tank. Then add a layer of pebbles, and then a layer of soil.

Dig up some little plants to put in your garden. Leave a little ball of soil around the roots. Mosses, ferns, and lichens will grow well in a hothouse garden. Or you may buy some tiny plants.

Arrange the plants in the soil and sprinkle with water. Put a little piece of cardboard on the rim of the bowl to hold the top glass up so air can get in. See Picture. Then place the piece of glass over the bowl.

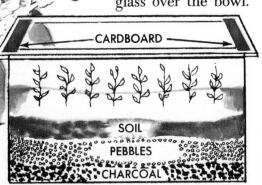

CARDBOARD

SOIL

PEBBLES

CHARCOAL

Set your hothouse garden near a sunny window. Sprinkle the garden every week. The water will rise up from the plants and stick on the top glass. Then it will fall on the plants like raindrops.

294

fun for the shut-in

A cabin made of paper logs, a spool that rolls up a ramp, and a snowstorm in a bottle are some of the kinds of games to play and things to do when you have to stay in bed.

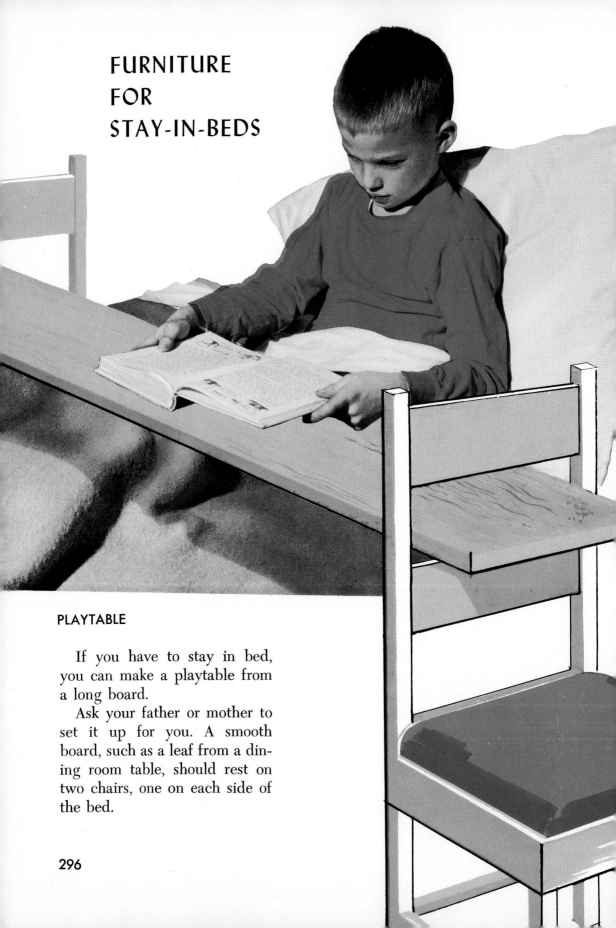

FURNITURE
FOR
STAY-IN-BEDS

PLAYTABLE

If you have to stay in bed, you can make a playtable from a long board.

Ask your father or mother to set it up for you. A smooth board, such as a leaf from a dining room table, should rest on two chairs, one on each side of the bed.

BESIDE-THE-BED SHELVES

Stack three small cardboard boxes of the same size side by side on top of each other. Fasten them together with masking tape or brown mailing tape. You can paint or decorate the top and sides with wall paper, pictures from magazines, or pieces of colored paper. The bottom shelf holds toys. Put flat things such as paper, coloring books, and cardboard on the middle shelf. On the top shelf you can put a fun tray (see below).

CARDBOARD FUN TRAY

A dress box, or a shallow cardboard box, can be made into a tray to hold things you want to play with. Put little cardboard boxes into it. Fill each little box with play materials like these: soda straws, pipe cleaners, yarn, star stickers, spools, wooden clothespins, crayons, paste, pencil, pieces of cloth, and ribbons. In one corner tie a bell to ring when you need mother.

BESIDE-THE-BED SHELVES

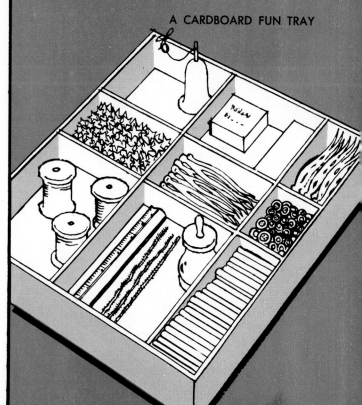

A CARDBOARD FUN TRAY

A good way to spend the time while you get well is to make a scrapbook or diary of special things that happen while you are in bed. Collect clippings from magazines and newspapers in a scrapbook, or write a story and draw pictures to go with it.

Use two sides of a soap-flakes box or two pieces of cardboard about the size of this page for covers. Paste paper over the cardboard and decorate it.

Cut sheets of paper for the pages of the book. They should be the size of the cardboard covers.

Punch holes along the side of the pages and the cardboard covers. Tie a ribbon through the holes as shown.

Spool Tractor

Materials

- an empty spool
- a wooden matchstick
- a small nail
- a small piece of soap
- a rubber band for the motor

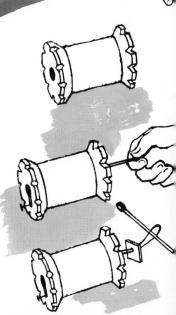

Spool tractors are easy to make and fun to play with. They roll by themselves and will even climb over the bumps on your bed.

Cut notches around the ends of the spool.

Hammer a small nail into the spool at one end.

Put a rubber band through the hole in the spool and hook one end of the band over the nail.

Cut a small piece of soap about as thick as a nickel. Make a hole in it so the rubber band will go through it.

Put the rubber band through the piece of soap, and slip a long matchstick through the loop.

Turn the matchstick around and around to wind up the rubber-band motor. Set the spool down on your bed or tabletop and watch it go.

Five-Pointed Star

To cut out a five-pointed star, just follow these steps. Start with a square sheet of paper. Fold it in half.

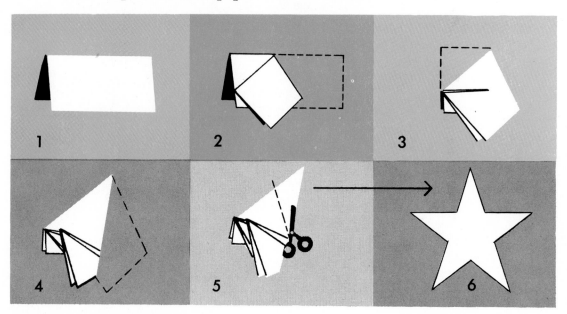

Paper Beads

Beads made from colored paper are attractive. You need colored paper, a piece of wire, and glue. Shellac the finished beads to make them hard.

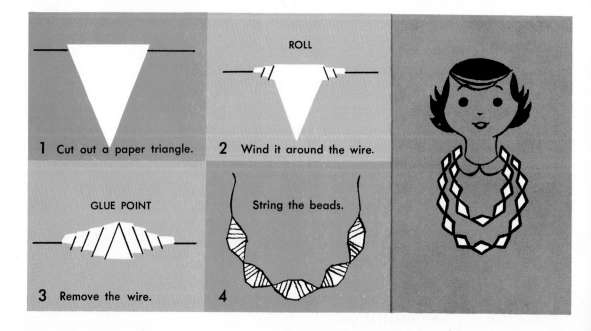

1 Cut out a paper triangle.

2 Wind it around the wire.

ROLL

GLUE POINT

3 Remove the wire.

String the beads.

4

Snowflake

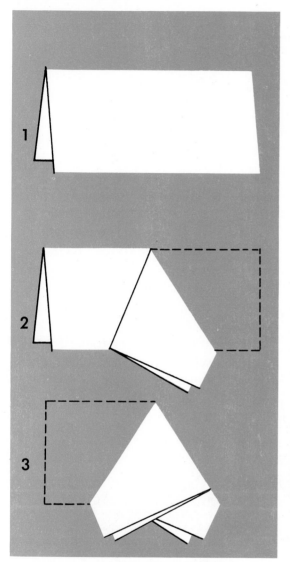

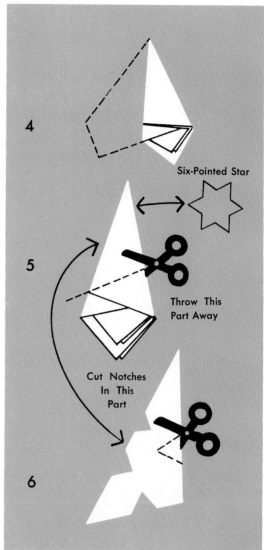

Six-Pointed Star

Throw This Part Away

Cut Notches In This Part

These steps make a six-pointed star. When you cut diamonds from the edges of the folded star, you make a design like a snowflake. Start with a square sheet of paper.

PAPER DOLLS

Here are two paper dolls you can dress.

Trace them on thin paper and paste the tracings on cardboard before you color them and cut them out.

It's easy to make clothes for the dolls. You can either trace the ones pictured here, or you can design your own. If you make your own, draw around the doll to get the right size.

Color the clothes. If you wish, you can decorate them by pasting on bits of lace and shiny paper.

Be sure you put tabs on all the clothes to hold them to the dolls.

You might like to draw dolls of your own. It is easiest to design clothes for paper dolls when their arms and legs stick straight out from their bodies.

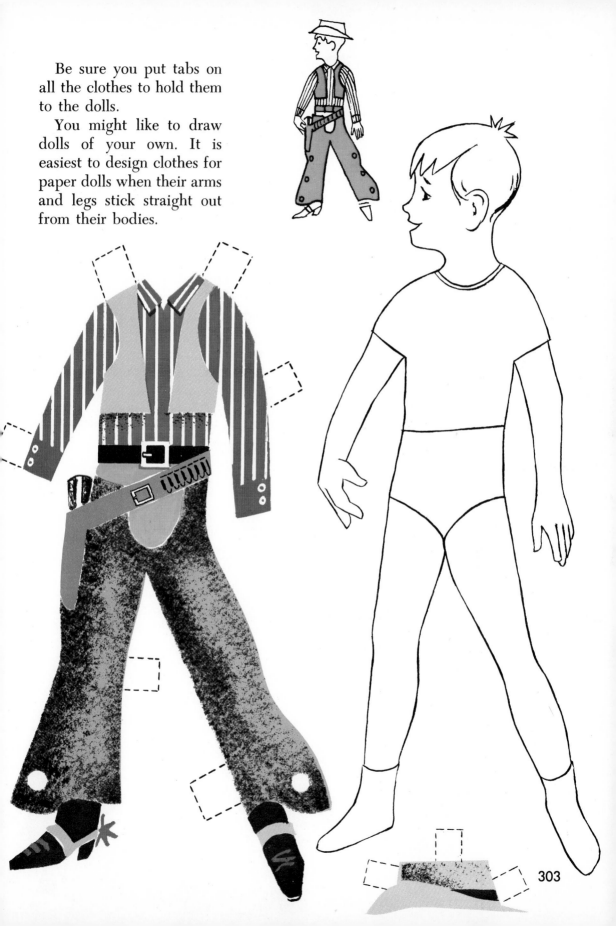

PAPER HOUSE

Make a paper house or a paper barn with paste, scissors, and a square piece of paper.

1

Fold the paper in half and then in half again the long way.

2

Fold it in half the short way and then in half again.

3–4

A			E
B			F
C			G
D			H

Unfold the paper and you will find that the creases in it make 16 squares.

Cut on the six heavy lines.

5

Paste Square C on top of Square B, and paste Square G on top of Square F.

Paste Square A halfway across Squares B and C. Paste Square D over Square A.

Paste Squares E and H over Squares F and G as in Step 6.

6–7

Cut a door and windows in the house or barn. Cut on the heavy lines. Fold on the dotted ones.

LOG CABIN

With a pencil, many sheets of paper, four pins, and paste you can make a pioneer log cabin.

Roll a sheet of notebook-size paper into a tube around a pencil, to make each log of the cabin. Paste the end of the paper to hold it in place. Pull out the pencil.

Build a cabin by stacking logs on top of each other. Paste in place.

Roll shorter logs, or cut down larger ones, to make peaks for the roof. Paste in place.

Use a large sheet of paper for the roof. Fold it in half.

Stick pins in the corners to hold the roof in place.

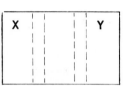

Use another large sheet of paper for the chimney. It should be wider than the cabin is high. Fold on the dotted lines.

Paste Y to X as shown.

Cut out overhang on one end of the roof, and paste the chimney to the end of the house. Cut out doors and windows after the paste is dry. Or paste paper doors and windows to the side of the cabin.

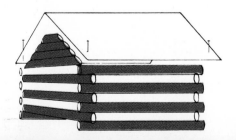

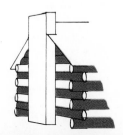

305

WINDOW-SILL GARDEN

Materials

- cottage-cheese cartons
- seeds from apples, oranges, melons, pumpkins, or squash
- pebbles
- soil
- moss or charcoal

(your mother can get them at a dime store)

Poke a hole in the bottom of each cottage-cheese carton. The hole will let excess water drain off. Set the cartons on saucers. Put pebbles in the bottom of each carton. Put a layer of moss or charcoal over the pebbles. Fill the rest with soil.

SEE IT GROW

Materials

- a blotter
- a drinking glass
- peas, beans, or radish seeds

Soak the seeds in water overnight.

Wet a blotter and line the inside of a glass with it. See Picture.

Poke the seeds down between the glass and the blotter.

Put four or five tablespoons of water into the glass each day to keep the blotter wet. Watch the roots, stems, and little leaves grow from the seeds.

SOIL

MOSS

PEBBLES

Drop five or six seeds on top of the soil in each carton. Sprinkle water on them every day. Some of the seeds will grow big and strong. Pull out the plants that do not grow well and throw them away. This gives the strong ones more room to grow.

WATCH IT SNOW

Materials
- a glass jar with a screw-on lid
- 2 tablespoons of moth flakes
- waterproof cement
- a little china statue

Cement a china statue to the inside of a jar lid and let it dry overnight. If you have no china figure, make a little doll or snowman by cementing buttons, spools, and beads together.

Fill the jar with water, almost to the top. Put moth flakes into the water.

Put cement inside the lid, where it screws on, and screw the lid to the jar tightly. Let it dry for a day.

Shake the jar and watch it "snow."

ANIMAL WALL SHADOWS

You can use your hands to shape all kinds of shadows on the wall, as long as there is enough sunlight or lamplight to make a shadow.

Try the animal shadows shown here. And if you experiment, you will soon be able to make others.

Move your fingers to open and close the animal's mouth, wiggle his ears, or flop his wings.

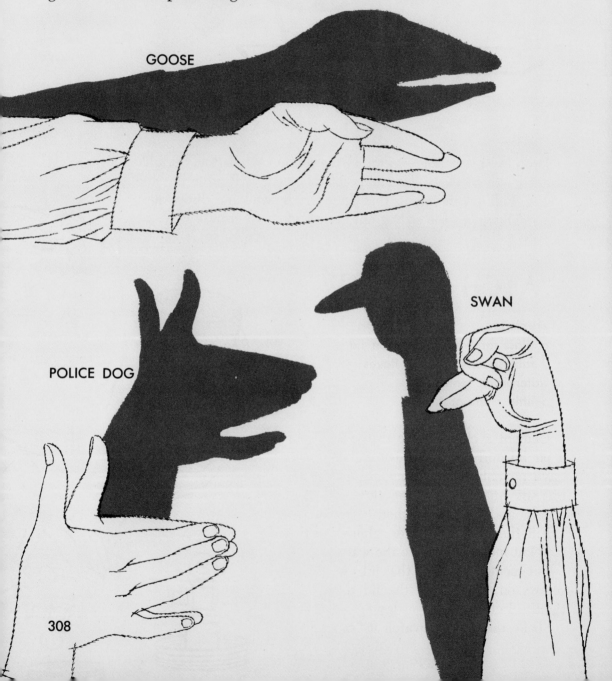

GOOSE

POLICE DOG

SWAN

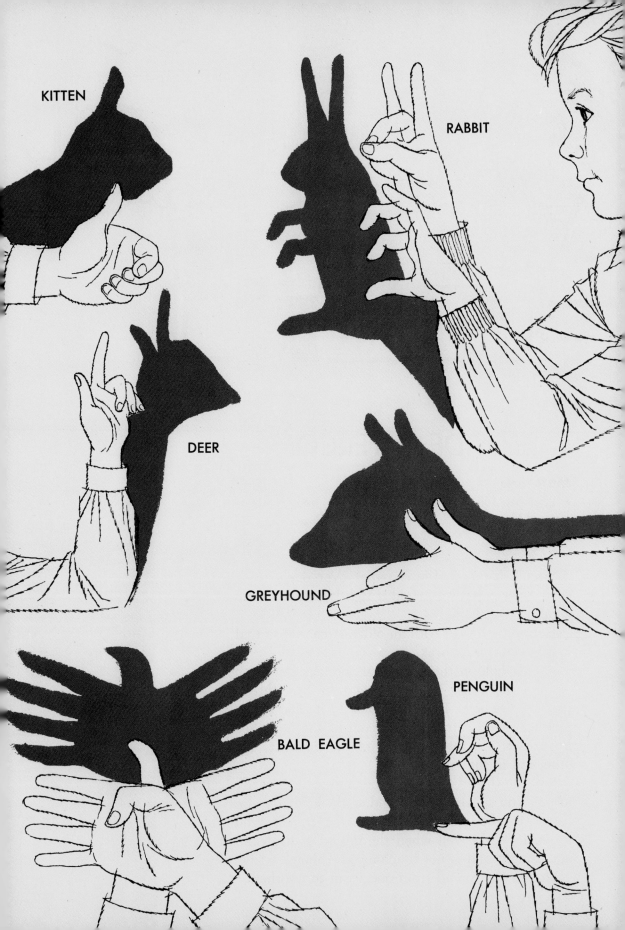

KITTEN

RABBIT

DEER

GREYHOUND

BALD EAGLE

PENGUIN

BEDSIDE INTERCOM

Materials

- 2 empty toilet-paper rolls
- 2 rubber bands
- wax paper
- heavy thread
- an old wax candle
- 2 toothpicks

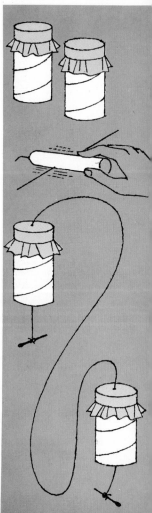

Stretch a piece of wax paper over one end of each toilet-paper roll. Hold it tightly in place with a rubber band.

Rub some thread with an old wax candle so that it is covered with wax.

Poke a hole in the middle of the wax paper on one of the rolls. Push one end of the thread through the hole. Tie a toothpick to it. The toothpick will keep it from pulling out of the hole. See Picture. Attach the other end of the thread to the other roll in the same way.

Pull the thread tight and your intercom is ready to use. You speak into one end, and somebody else listens at the other end. When he speaks, you listen. It works well when the thread is stretched out straight and is not touching anything.

Stretch the thread from one room to another.

SECRET WRITING

You can write all kinds of secret messages that won't show on paper. Only those persons who know how to make the writing appear will be able to read them. Write your message in milk, lemon juice, or onion juice. You can write it with a thin brush or a clean pen on any kind of paper.

When the milk or juice dries it will not show, and the paper will look blank. The message will show if you hold it over a warm radiator or light bulb.

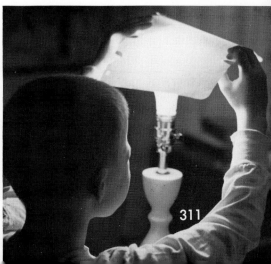

SIT-BACK-AND-PLAY GAMES

A SPIN
BASEBALL GAME

Materials
• a large sheet of cardboard   • crayons   • a paper fastener

Cut a large square from a sheet of cardboard.

With crayons, draw a baseball diamond on it like the one in the picture. Mark the home plate and the three bases. Outside the baselines print home run, ball, double, out, triple, strike, single, as shown. In the center of the diamond draw a pitcher's mound.

From the left-over cardboard cut a spinner shaped like a baseball bat or like an arrow. See Picture.

Poke a hole through the center of the spinner and through the center of the pitcher's mound. Attach the spinner to the pitcher's mound with a paper fastener. Be sure it can spin easily.

Follow regular baseball rules when you play. If you play by yourself, spin for both teams.

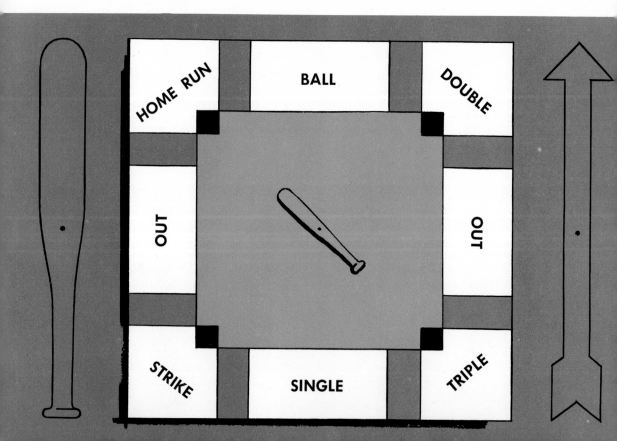

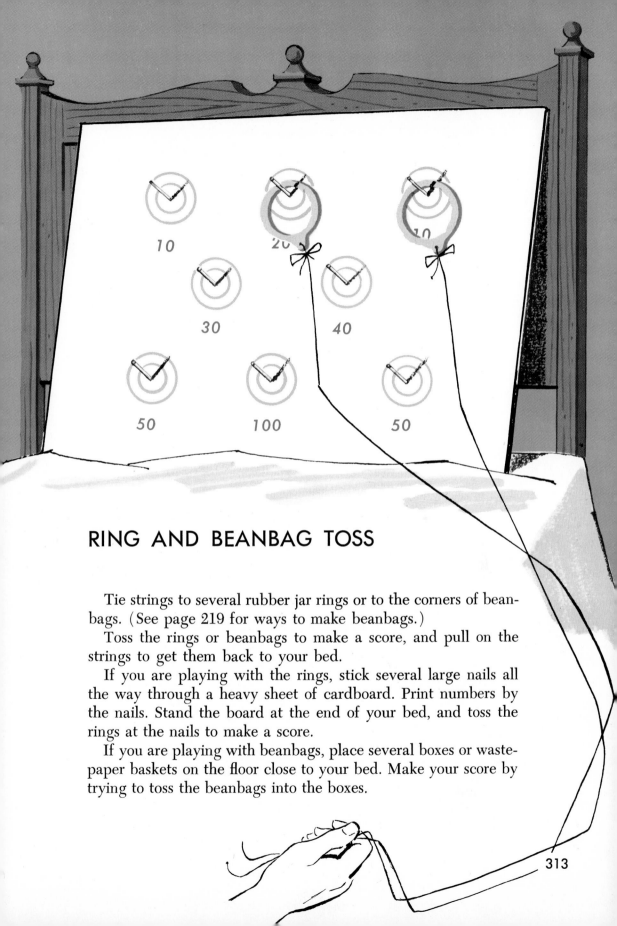

RING AND BEANBAG TOSS

Tie strings to several rubber jar rings or to the corners of bean-bags. (See page 219 for ways to make beanbags.)

Toss the rings or beanbags to make a score, and pull on the strings to get them back to your bed.

If you are playing with the rings, stick several large nails all the way through a heavy sheet of cardboard. Print numbers by the nails. Stand the board at the end of your bed, and toss the rings at the nails to make a score.

If you are playing with beanbags, place several boxes or waste-paper baskets on the floor close to your bed. Make your score by trying to toss the beanbags into the boxes.

Yarn Doll

A

B

C

Materials

- yarn
- cardboard

Yarn dolls are easy to make and fun to play with. You can make them any size you wish.

Wrap yarn around a piece of cardboard. The cardboard should be as long as you want the doll to be. Cut the strands at one end.

The end where the strands are not cut will be the doll's head. Tie a piece of yarn around the neck.

Divide the strands for the two arms. Cut the ends to make them shorter than the rest of the strands.

Tie pieces of yarn at the end of the arms and body.

Divide the strands for the legs, and tie pieces of yarn around the feet.

D

E

the shape of things

Some shapes and designs are as flat as a sheet of paper. Others are as thick as a telephone pole. You see flat designs and thick designs everywhere. The next pages show you some of the things you can make and do with many kinds of shapes and designs.

WHAT'S THE DESIGN?

Some designs look like Christmas trees, and some look like sheets of paper. Some designs look like pennies, and some even look like buildings.

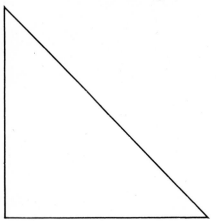

This design looks like a paper napkin folded kitty-cornered. The design is called a triangle. It has three sides. The sides meet and form corners. The corners are called angles. A triangle has three angles. All triangles have three sides and three angles. *Tri* means three.

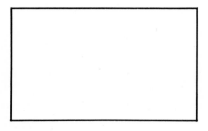

This design looks like a sheet of paper. It has four sides. The design is called a rectangle. *Rect* means right. An angle is called a right angle when its sides make a square corner. The four angles of the rectangle are right angles.

This design is a rectangle, too. It has four sides and four corners or angles. But it is a special kind of rectangle called a square. It's called a square because all four sides are the same length.

This design looks like a penny. The design is called a circle. It has no sides and no corners or angles. It just goes all around and meets itself where it began.

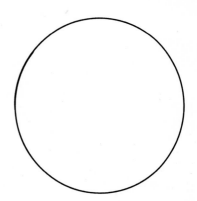

This design looks like a famous building in Washington, D.C. The design has five sides and five corners or angles. It's called a pentagon. The building in Washington, D.C., is called the Pentagon. *Penta* means five and *gon* means angle.

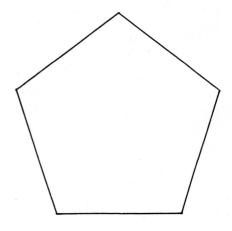

All these designs are as flat as they can be, and they have length and width. We call these flat designs planes.

FROM ONE DESIGN TO ANOTHER

Can you turn this square into a rectangle? You might think it's impossible, but it really isn't. Here's what you do. Divide the square into three parts—A, B, and C. If you fit parts A, B, and C together like this, you can make a rectangle from a square.

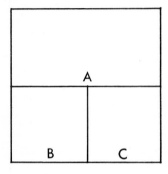

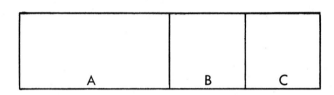

Now try to make a triangle from this square. Divide the square into two parts—A and B. Fit the parts together as shown below, and you can make a triangle from a square.

Make your own pattern out of construction paper or thin cardboard. Then, see how many other ways you can make a rectangle from a square, or a triangle from a square.

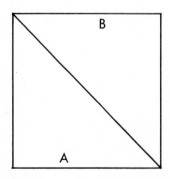

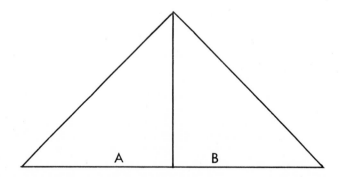

FOLD
A
PENTAGON

Can you take a strip of paper as long as a ruler and turn it into a star? First, carefully tie the strip of paper into a loose knot. Then, flatten the knot with your fist. You will have a design with five sides called a pentagon. Fold one end of the strip over the pentagon. Hold it up to a strong light. And what do you see? A five-pointed star!

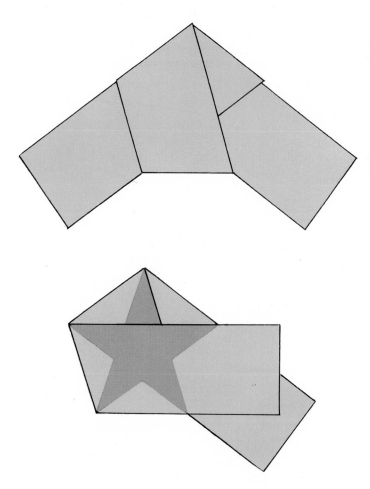

SHAPES FROM TRIANGLES AND SQUARES

Triangles and squares are flat designs. But you can use them to make shapes that are not flat. Sometimes they can even stand up by themselves. These shapes are called solid shapes. A solid shape has length, width, and thickness.

Here's how to make a solid shape that will stand up by itself. Trace this triangle design for your pattern. **1.** Cut out the tracing. **2.** Trace your pattern on construction paper. **3.** Cut out the pattern. **4.** Fold the paper on the dotted lines. **5.** Fold the tabs over and paste them down. Now you have a shape that looks like this:

We call this shape a pyramid. A pyramid is a solid shape. Long ago, people in Egypt built huge pyramids of stone.

Now trace this square shape for your pattern. Follow the five steps listed above. And you have a shape that looks like this:

We call this shape a cube. A cube is a solid shape. Water freezes into ice cubes in an ice-cube tray.

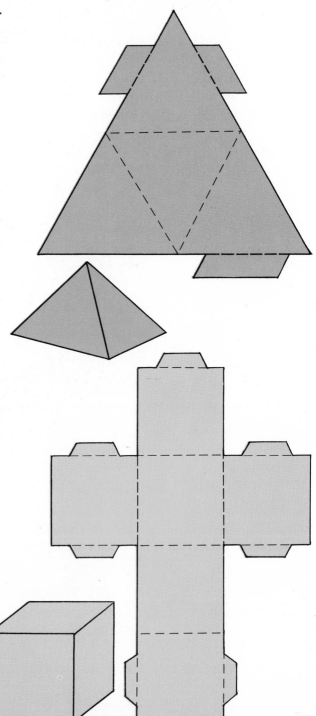

You can combine triangles and squares and get still other solid shapes. Trace this triangle and square design. Follow the five steps listed on the facing page. When you're through, you have a shape that looks like the one in the picture below. We call this shape a polyhedron. *Poly* means many, and *hedron* means sides. "Polyhedron" always means a solid shape with many sides.

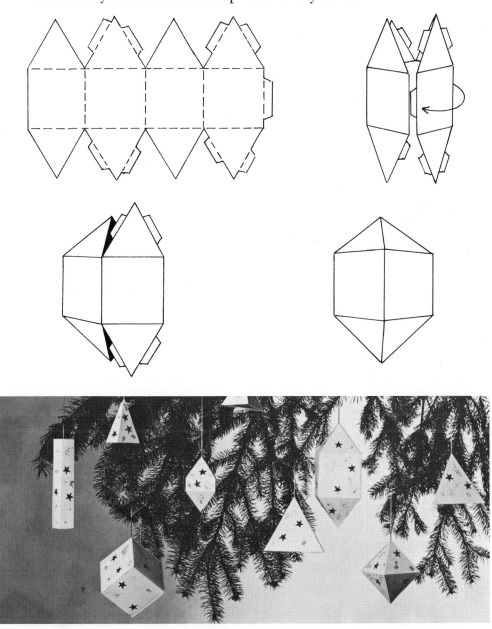

You can make mobiles, Christmas tree ornaments, and party decorations with your pyramids, cubes, and polyhedrons. Loop them with string and hang them up.

PUZZLES

There are crossword puzzles and jigsaw puzzles, number puzzles, and letter puzzles. Now here are some puzzles with triangles, rectangles, squares, and circles. Use tracing paper and see how many of them you can do.

TRIANGLE PUZZLE

Can you trace these triangles without going over a line, and without lifting your pencil from the paper?

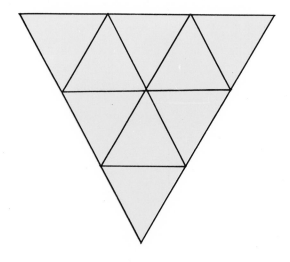

RECTANGLE AND TRIANGLE PUZZLE

This puzzle looks like an open envelope with the flap up. Can you trace the drawing without going over a line more than once, and without lifting your pencil from the paper?

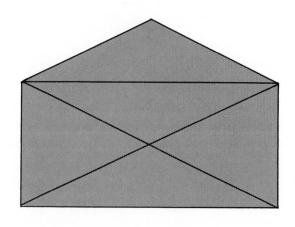

322

CIRCLE AND HALF-MOONS PUZZLE

Can you trace the circle and half moons without lifting your pencil from the paper?

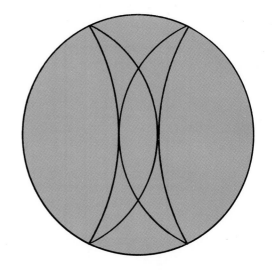

SQUARE AND RECTANGLE PUZZLE

A farmer left a plot of land to four sons. The plot was shaped like this:

Can you divide this plot of land so that each son would have a plot of land the same size and the same shape?

The answers to these puzzles are on page 328.

PUZZLES TO MAKE

You can find some puzzles in books and magazines you have at home, and you can buy some puzzles in stores. But sometimes it's more fun to make your own puzzles. Can you make and do these square and triangle puzzles?

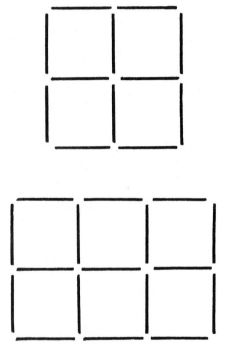

TOOTHPICK PUZZLES

First, make four squares out of twelve toothpicks, like the ones in the picture. Then try to take away two toothpicks so that you have only two squares. Now make six squares with seventeen toothpicks. See Picture. Can you take away six toothpicks so that you have only two squares?

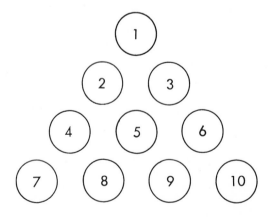

COIN PUZZLE

Make a triangle with ten coins of the same kind, placed like the circles in the picture. Can you move only three coins so that the triangle will be upside down—so that the point will point down instead of up?

The answers to these puzzles are on page 328.

PICTURE PUZZLE

This picture puzzle is made of many designs. How many squares, rectangles, triangles, pentagons, and circles can you find?

MYSTERY PAPER RING

How many paper rings do you think you would have if you cut *one* paper ring in half? One? Two?

Cut a strip of paper about one inch wide and about as long as two rulers. Loop the strip into a ring. Give the strip a half twist before pasting the ends of the strip together. See Picture.

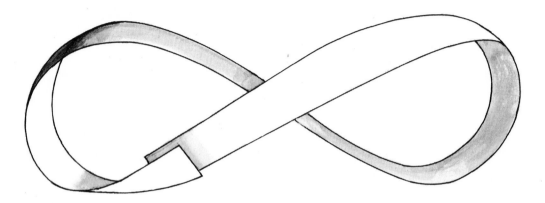

Poke a hole in the middle of the strip with scissors. Start to cut along the middle of the strip. Be sure to follow the curve of the paper. When you get back to the starting point, what do you have? Not *two* rings as you thought you'd have. You have one big ring, instead!

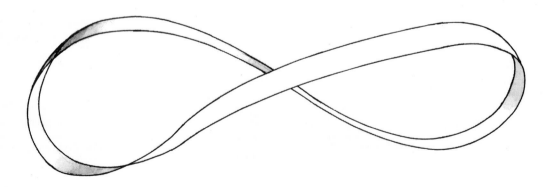

You know what happens when you cut a mystery ring. What do you think will happen if you try to color one side red and the other side green?

Make another mystery ring. Start coloring one side red. Keep coloring until you get back to where you started, so that you know one side of the paper ring is red.

Now, you're ready to color the other side green. But, what happened? You have no place to color it green. That is because the mystery ring seems to have only one side. This seemingly one-sided ring is called a Möbius strip.

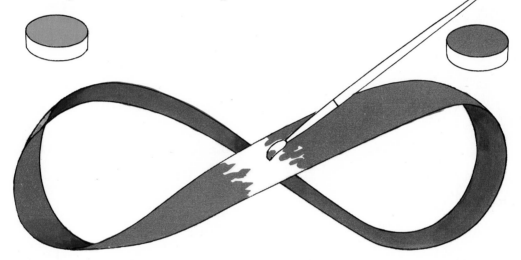

Make another Möbius strip. But this time cut it in thirds. You'll get another surprise!

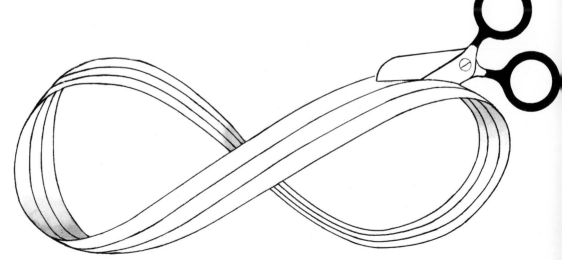

ANSWERS TO PUZZLES

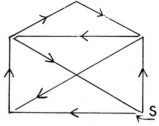

Rectangle and Triangle Puzzle

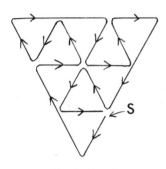

Triangle Puzzle

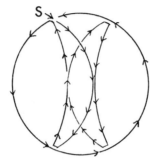

Circle and Half-Moons Puzzle

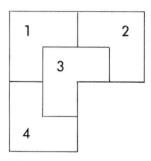

Square and Rectangle Puzzle

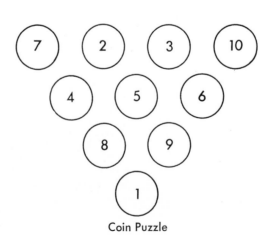

Toothpick Puzzles

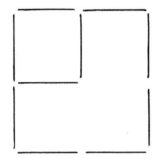

Coin Puzzle

Skill Development Guide

The natural impulses of children, when intelligently guided, can lead them to gain valuable experiences and desirable social habits. The skills which may be developed and guided through the use of this book are arranged in this Skill Development Guide into natural activity areas—manipulative, investigative, artistic, social, and others.

Artistic

Clay modeling: 68–81, 86–87, 90–91, 200–201
Color discrimination: 40–55, 66
Drawing: 10–11, 16–19, 26, 34–35, 38–51, 58–63, 84–85, 127, 146–147, 150, 195–199, 204–205, 210, 212–213, 286, 302–303, 312–313
Music interest: 20–23
Painting: 40–49, 74–75, 90–92, 98–101, 106–108, 132–133, 136–137, 200–203, 205–206
Papier-mâché modeling: 88–92, 206
Picture making: 42–61, 134, 208–209

Body coordination

Games: 124–127, 130, 266–267
Stunts: 152–157, 308–309
Tumbling: 154–157

Domestic arts

Braiding: 220
Cooking: 234–235, 237–256
Sewing: 200–201, 208–219

Investigation

Camping: 221, 226–227, 230–236
Collecting: 266–267, 274–285
Hiking: 221–225, 228–229, 236
Measuring: 34–37, 237–256
Nature study: 264–267, 282–285, 294
Tours: 262–265, 268–269, 272

Manipulation

Carving: 64–65, 84–85
Cutting: 8–11, 14–19, 25, 28–31, 34–38, 58, 82, 92, 127, 132–137, 142–150, 158, 184–188, 190–191, 194–195, 197–205, 209, 212–219, 286, 298–305, 312, 314, 326–327
Fastening: 12–17, 22–23, 26–29, 34–35, 82–83, 134–135, 142–143, 184–187
Folding: 10–11, 25, 36–37, 138–141, 146–150, 300–301, 304–305
Hammering: 20–21, 24, 96–107, 299
Pasting (Gluing): 56–61, 66, 78–79, 86–87, 92, 98–105, 108, 134–139, 142–149, 188, 190–191, 195–199, 286, 289, 298, 304–305, 307
Sawing: 96–101, 104–105, 286
Tying: 6–7, 17, 28–29, 82, 83, 106–107, 144–145, 164–165, 204–205, 284, 310, 313–314

Organization

Dramatics: 173–183, 188–189, 192
Exhibitions: 176–177, 180–181, 193–206
Parties: 110–130

Personal responsibility

Collecting: 266–267, 274–285
Gardening: 294, 306–307
Pets: 290–293

Social

Games: 116–130, 258–261, 266–267, 270–271
Magic (Tricks): 158–174
Parties: 109–130

Illustration Acknowledgments

The publishers of *Childcraft* gratefully acknowledge the following artists, photographers, publishers, agencies, and corporations for illustrations in this volume. Page numbers refer to two-page spreads. The words "(left)," "(center)," "(top)," "(bottom)," and "(right)," indicate position on the spread. All illustrations are the exclusive property of the publishers of *Childcraft* unless names are marked with an asterisk (*).

1: Robert Keys
5: Paul McNear
6-7: John Henry
8-9: John M. Bolt, Jr.
10-11: Kong Wu

12-13: Robert Kresin
14-21: John M. Bolt, Jr.
22-23: Robert Kresin
24-25: Cosmo Demiduc
26-27: *(left)* sculpture, Suzi Hawes; photo, James H. Brown; *(right)* Cosmo Demiduc
28-29: art, John Henry and Paul McNear
30-31: Cosmo Demiduc
32-33: art, Kong Wu; photo, Alfa Studios
34-35: art, Ed Fitzgerald; photo, Donald Stebbing
36-37: Ed Fitzgerald
38-39: *(left)* Luke Doheny; *(right)* Carl Yates
40-41: photo, Donald Stebbing; art, Charles Klingbeil
42-43: Ed Fitzgerald
44-45: *(bottom left)* photo, Pinney, Monkmeyer *; art, Suzi Hawes; *(right)* photo, James H. Brown
46-47: *(left)* photo, James H. Brown, art, Wayne Gallagher; *(right)* art, Suzi Hawes and Wayne Gallagher
48-49: *(top left and top right)* John Erdos; *(bottom left and right)* Suzi Hawes
50-51: *(left)* John Erdos; *(right)* Suzi Hawes
52-53: Suzi Hawes
54-55: *(top)* Suzi Hawes; *(bottom)* Robert Kresin
56-57: Suzi Hawes

330

Index

This index is an alphabetical list of the important topics covered in this book. It will help you find information given in both words *and* pictures. To help you understand what an entry means, there is often a helping word in parentheses. For example, **appliqué** (sewing). If there is information in both words and pictures, you will see the words *with pictures* after the page number. If there is *only* a picture, you will see the word *picture* before the page number. If you do not find what you want in this index, please go to the General Index in Volume 15, which is a key to all of the books.